河南省哲社规划年度项目(2018BJY018)成果
河南中医药大学2019年度思想政治教育研究项目(HZYSZ2019-16)成果

中国古代教育智慧
（汉英对照）

HIGHLIGHTS ON EDUCATION IN ANCIENT CHINESE CLASSICS
(Chinese-English)

肖莉莉　张夔真　孙俊芳　编著

东南大学出版社
SOUTHEAST UNIVERSITY PRESS
·南京·

内容提要

中国自古以来就非常看重教育,而且教育的理念广博而宏大。大到君王治理天下,教化万民,小到个人修身养性,均有涉及。

本书整理搜集了中国传统典籍及古代名人有关教育的名言若干条,按朝代分类,以让现代人充分领略中国古代教育智慧的闪光点。本书为每一句(段)名言都提供了参考译文,以方便英语国家的人阅读。

图书在版编目(CIP)数据

中国古代教育智慧:汉英对照 / 肖莉莉,张巽真,孙俊芳编著. -- 南京:东南大学出版社,2020.12(2021.1重印)
 ISBN 978-7-5641-9210-5

Ⅰ. ①中… Ⅱ. ①肖… ②张… ③孙… Ⅲ. ①教育思想—中国—古代—汉、英 Ⅳ. ①G40-092.2

中国版本图书馆 CIP 数据核字(2020)第 223384 号

中国古代教育智慧(汉英对照)
ZHONGGUO GUDAI JIAOYU ZHIHUI(HANYING DUIZHAO)

编　　著	肖莉莉　张巽真　孙俊芳	责任编辑	刘　坚
电　　话	(025)83793329／QQ:635353748	电子邮箱	liu-jian@seu.edu.cn
出版发行	东南大学出版社	出 版 人	江建中
地　　址	南京市四牌楼2号	邮　　编	210096
销售电话	83794561/83794174/83794121/83795801/83792174/83795802/57711295(传真)		
网　　址	http://www.seupress.com	电子邮箱	press@seupress.com
经　　销	全国各地新华书店	印　　刷	广东虎彩云印刷有限公司
开　　本	787 mm×1092 mm　1/16	印　　张	10.25　字　数　250千字
版　　次	2020年12月第1版	印　　次	2021年1月第2次印刷
书　　号	ISBN 978-7-5641-9210-5		
定　　价	50.00元		

＊ 未经许可,本书内文字不得以任何方式转载、演绎,违者必究。

＊ 本社图书若有印装质量问题,请直接与营销部联系。电话:025-83791830。

序
Preface

　　中华文化平静而舒缓的历史长河滋养了无数心灵丰富而知识广博的精神贵族,他们以细腻的笔触和独到的见解,为后人留下了许多隽永的篇章和富于启迪的文字,其中相当多的部分是和教育有关的。这些文字虽然有着各自的历史局限性,但在"快餐文化"充斥的今天,依然闪烁着智慧的光芒。无论是永恒的经典"四书五经",还是荀子的《劝学》、老子的《道德经》、韩愈的《师说》等教育名篇,都已经成为今天教育领域取之不竭的源头活水,滋养着一代又一代的学者和教育家。

　　中国自古以来就非常看重教育,而且教育的理念广博而宏大。大到君王治理天下,教化万民,小到个人修身养性,均有涉及。因此《大学》中说"大学之道,在明明德,在亲民,在止于至善。"

　　本书对这些教育智慧进行了梳理和归纳,原来计划按照教育的不同方面进行分类,但是发现涵盖的方面太多太广,后改为按照历代典籍的时间顺序进行排列,主要收取了(但不局限于)以下几个方面的教育名言:

　　君王德治天下。如:"居宠思危,罔不惟畏,弗畏入畏。推贤让能,庶官乃和,不和政庞。""蓄疑败谋,怠忽荒政。""若网在纲,有条而不紊;若农服田力穑,乃亦有秋。"(《尚书》)"古之欲明明德于天下者,先治其国;欲治其国者,先齐其家;欲齐其家者,先修其身;欲修其身者,先正其心;欲正其心者,先诚其意;欲诚其意者,先致其知,致知在格物。"(《大学》)

　　戒骄矜自满。如:"企者不立;跨者不行;自见者不明;自是者不彰;自伐者无功;自矜者不长。""知人者智;自知者明。胜人者有力,胜己者强。知足者富,强行者有志。不失其所者久,死而不亡者寿。"(《道德经》)

　　要恬淡节制。如"故智者之养生也,必顺四时而适寒暑,和喜怒而安居处,节阴阳而调刚柔。如是则僻邪不至,长生久视。""外不劳形于事,内无思想之患,以恬愉为务,以自得为功。"(《黄帝内经》)

　　医学教育:"非其人勿教,非其真勿授,是谓得道。"(《黄帝内经》)

　　人际交往的原则:"为人君,止于仁;为人臣,止于敬;为人子,止于孝;为人父,止于慈;与国人交,止于信。"《大学》

　　有些名句是大家耳熟能详的,却不一定明确其出处,如:"仓廪实而知礼节,衣食足则知荣辱。"(《管子·牧民》)汤之《盘铭》曰:"苟日新,日日新,又日新。"《康诰》曰:"作新民。"《诗》曰:"周虽旧邦,其命维新。""是故君子无所不用其极。"(《大学》)

　　还有些已经化为成语至今在用的。如"有其善,丧厥善;矜其能,丧厥功。惟事事,乃

其有备,有备无患。""夙夜罔或不勤,不矜细行,终累大德。为山九仞,功亏一篑。"(《尚书》)

我们必须承认中国古代的教育思想也有一定的局限性,比如缺乏严密的逻辑论证和系统的理论体系,但是这些古老的教育智慧已经成为我们对外交往的一张文化名片,而且依然给我们今天教育领域的创新和发展带来灵感和启示。

在此意义上,这本书似是一扇窗,可以让现代读者既领略到古代的教育智慧,又不至于对浩如烟海的经典巨著望而生畏;因其提供了译文,不仅使中国读者得以与其他文化的人们分享这些思想,又能使外国留学生在学习汉语的同时得以欣赏中国的古代教育哲学。所以,这本书似乎又是一架桥,贯通古今,连接中西,使任何徜徉其间的人都能风景遍览,畅意而归。

孙俊芳

2020 年 3 月 25 日

目录
Contents

一、先秦时期 *Pre-Qin Period* ··· 001
  （一）《周易》*The Book of Changes* ·· 001
  （二）《尚书》*Shangshu* ··· 004
  （三）《诗经》*The Book of Poetry* ··· 011
  （四）《左传》*Zuo Zhuan（Chronicle of Zuo）* ······················· 013
  （五）《黄帝内经》*Huangdi Neijing（Inner Canon of the Yellow Emporor）* ··· 014
  （六）《道德经》*Tao Te Ching* ··· 015
  （七）《管子》*Guanzi* ·· 017
  （八）《论语》*The Analects of Confucius* ······························ 021
  （九）《墨子》*Mozi* ··· 034
  （十）《孟子》*Mencius* ··· 038
  （十一）《庄子》*Zhuangzi* ·· 045
  （十二）《荀子》*Xunzi* ··· 053
  （十三）《礼记》*The Book of Rites* ······································· 061
  （十四）《大学》*The Great Learning* ···································· 062
  （十五）《中庸》*Doctrine of the Mean* ································· 076
  （十六）《韩非子》*Han Feizi* ·· 088
  （十七）《吕氏春秋》*Spring and Autumn Annals of Lü Buwei* ············· 089

二、两汉三国时期 *The Han Dynasties and the Three Kingdoms Period* ········ 093
  （一）《汉乐府》*Yue Fu Poems of the Han Dynasty* ·············· 093
  （二）《韩诗外传》*Hanshi Waizhuan* ···································· 093
  （三）《淮南子》*Huainanzi* ··· 094

（四）《史记》Records of the Grand Historian ……………………… 094

　　（五）《大戴礼记》Elder Dai's Book of Rites ……………………… 095

　　（六）《说苑·建本》Garden of Anecdotes ………………………… 095

　　（七）《汉书》History of the Han Dynasty ………………………… 096

　　（八）《潜夫论》A Treatise on the Latent Man …………………… 096

　　（九）《中论》On Appropriateness ………………………………… 097

　　（十）《诸葛亮集·诫子书》Collected Works of Zhuge Liang …… 097

　　（十一）《万机论》On State Affairs ………………………………… 098

三、魏晋南北朝时期 Period of Wei, Jin, Southern and Northern Dynasties …… 099

　　（一）《三国志》History of the Three Kingdoms ………………… 099

　　（二）陶渊明诗文 Poems & Writings of Tao Yuanming ………… 099

　　（三）《世说新语》A New Account of Tales of the World ……… 100

　　（四）《文心雕龙》The Literary Mind and the Carving of Dragons …… 102

　　（五）《颜氏家训》Admonition for the Yan Clan ………………… 105

四、唐宋时期 Period of the Tang and Song Dynasties ………………… 110

　　（一）王之涣 Wang Zhihuan ………………………………………… 110

　　（二）李白 Li Bai …………………………………………………… 110

　　（三）杜甫 Du Fu …………………………………………………… 111

　　（四）孟郊 Meng Jiao ……………………………………………… 113

　　（五）杜荀鹤 Du Xunhe …………………………………………… 114

　　（六）陆游 Lu You ………………………………………………… 115

　　（七）吴兢 Wu Jing ………………………………………………… 117

　　（八）韩愈 Han Yu ………………………………………………… 118

　　（九）刘禹锡 Liu Yuxi ……………………………………………… 118

　　（十）严羽 Yan Yu ………………………………………………… 118

　　（十一）范仲淹 Fan Zhongyan …………………………………… 119

　　（十二）司马光 Sima Guang ……………………………………… 119

　　（十三）张载 Zhang Zai …………………………………………… 119

　　（十四）程颐 Cheng Yi …………………………………………… 122

(十五) 苏轼 *Su Shi* 124

　　(十六) 欧阳修 *Ouyang Xiu* 125

　　(十七) 黄庭坚 *Huang Tingjian* 128

　　(十八) 晁说之 *Chao Yuezhi* 128

　　(十九) 朱熹 *Zhu Xi* 129

　　(二十) 张孝祥 *Zhang Xiaoxiang* 132

　　(二十一) 杨时 *Yang Shi* 132

　　(二十二) 陆九渊 *Lu Jiuyuan* 136

　　(二十三) 罗大经 *Luo Dajing* 136

五、元明清时期 *Period of the Yuan, Ming and Qing Dynasties* 137

　　(一) 关汉卿 *Guan Hanqing* 137

　　(二) 宋濂 *Song Lian* 137

　　(三) 罗贯中 *Luo Guanzhong* 137

　　(四) 于谦 *Yu Qian* 138

　　(五) 文嘉 *Wen Jia* 138

　　(六) 王守仁 *Wang Shouren* 138

　　(七) 王延相 *Wang Yanxiang* 139

　　(八) 洪应明 *Hong Yingming* 139

　　(九) 《增广贤文》 *Zengguang Xianwen* 139

　　(十) 李贽 *Li Zhi* 141

　　(十一) 王骥德 *Wang Jide* 142

　　(十二) 董其昌 *Dong Qichang* 142

　　(十三) 黄宗羲 *Huang Zongxi* 143

　　(十四) 顾炎武 *Gu Yanwu* 143

　　(十五) 王夫之 *Wang Fuzhi* 143

　　(十六) 朱柏庐 *Zhu Bailu* 144

　　(十七) 张履祥 *Zhang Lüxiang* 144

　　(十八) 颜元 *Yan Yuan* 145

　　(十九) 李毓秀 *Li Yuxiu* 145

　　(二十) 张潮 *Zhang Chao* 146

(二十一) 张伯行 Zhang Boxing …… 147

(二十二) 彭端淑 Peng Duanshu …… 149

(二十三) 刘岩 Liu Yan …… 149

(二十四) 袁枚 Yuan Mei …… 150

(二十五) 方东树 Fang Dongshu …… 150

(二十六) 龚自珍 Gong Zizhen …… 150

(二十七) 魏源 Wei Yuan …… 151

(二十八) 曾国藩 Zeng Guofan …… 151

(二十九) 刘蓉 Liu Rong …… 152

参考文献 Works Cited …… 153

一 先秦时期
Pre-Qin Period

(一)《周易》
The Book of Changes

1 【原文】天行健,君子以自强不息。

《周易·乾》

【今译】天的运行刚强劲健、永不止息,君子当效法天道之健,发奋图强、不断进取。

(肖莉莉 译)

【英译】Just as heaven moves forever vigorously, Junzi(a man of virtue) should renew strength and strive hard unceasingly.

(肖莉莉 译)

2 【原文】地势坤,君子以厚德载物。

《周易·坤》

【今译】大地的气势厚实和顺,君子应效法大地,用广大博厚的德泽容载万物。

(肖莉莉 译)

【英译】Kun symbolizes the thick and receptive earth which gives birth to all things, likewise, Junzi(a man of virtue) should hold the outer world with great virtue.

(肖莉莉 译)

3 【原文】积善之家,必有余庆;积不善之家,必有余殃。

《周易·坤》

【今译】积德行善的人家,先辈遗留的福泽必将造福子孙;积累恶行的人家,先辈留下的祸患必会殃及子孙。

(肖莉莉 译)

【英译】A family that accumulates goodness is sure to have abundant happiness for its offsprings; whereas a family that accumulates evil is bound to leave behind endless miseries.

(肖莉莉 译)

4 【原文】蒙,亨。匪我求童蒙,童蒙求我。

《周易·蒙》

【今译】蒙卦,象征童蒙。蒙昧加以引导,所以亨通。并非老师要求蒙童接受教育,而是蒙童应该主动地向老师请教。

(肖莉莉 译)

【英译】Meng indicates prosperity for it symbolizes fighting off ignorance by the commencement of education. It is not I who ask the ignorant and uneducated to accept education, but the ignorant and uneducated should come to me for education.

(肖莉莉 译)

5 【原文】初筮告,再三渎,渎则不告。

《周易·蒙》

【今译】初次前来占筮祈问便施以教诲,接二连三地占筮,便是对占筮的亵渎,如此便不再施教。

(肖莉莉 译)

【英译】For the first divination, information should be given; for the second or the third time, no information could be passed since it is profane.

(肖莉莉 译)

6 【原文】蒙以养正,圣功也。

《周易·蒙》

【今译】童稚蒙昧的时候就应当教以养正育德,此乃造就圣人的成功之路。

(肖莉莉 译)

【英译】If the cultivation of moral character in a child at the time of ignorance never slackens, cultivation of a sage is sure to follow.

(肖莉莉 译)

7 【原文】君子以果行育德。

《周易·蒙》

【今译】君子当果断行动来培育美德。

(肖莉莉 译)

【英译】Thus Junzi(a man of virtue) fosters his character by putting one's foot down in all that he does.

(肖莉莉 译)

8 【原文】发蒙,利用刑人。

《周易·蒙》

【今译】启发蒙昧的人,利于树立正面典型来教育人。

(肖莉莉 译)

【英译】To enlighten the ignorant can set a good example for education.

(肖莉莉 译)

9 【原文】击蒙;不利为寇,利御寇。

《周易·蒙》

【今译】惊醒愚昧、启发蒙稚,不宜采用攻击性的暴烈方式,而宜于采用防御性的和缓行为。

(肖莉莉 译)

【英译】In smiting ignorance, advantage will not come from violent aggressive measures, but from moderate defensive measures.

(肖莉莉 译)

10 【原文】君子以见善则迁,有过则改。

《周易·益》

【今译】君子见了善行就追随,有了过错就改正。

(肖莉莉 译)

【英译】Junzi(a man of virtue) imitates goodness when he sees it, and abandons faults when he has it.

(肖莉莉 译)

11 【原文】二人同心,其利断金;同心之言,其臭如兰。

《周易·系辞上》

【今译】只要两个人同心协力,就能发挥很大的力量,其锋利程度足以切金断玉。同心同德的人发表一致的意见,其气味就像兰草那样芬芳。

(肖莉莉 译)

【英译】When two men are of one heart, they will gather enough strength with which metal can be cut; when two men are of one mind, their speeches will be as fragrant as orchids.

(肖莉莉 译)

12 【原文】君子藏器于身,待时而动。

《周易·系辞下》

【今译】君子有卓越的才能而不炫耀,只在必要的时刻才施展出来。

(肖莉莉 译)

【英译】Junzi(a man of virtue) doesn't show off his talent but gives full play to it when needed.

(肖莉莉 译)

13 【原文】有天地,然后万物生焉。………物生必蒙,故授之以《蒙》。

《周易·序卦传》

【今译】有了天地以后,万物开始萌生。………万物初生必然蒙昧无知,所以接着是象征此意的《蒙》卦。

(肖莉莉 译)

【英译】There are heaven and earth first from which all lives spring. ... All newly-born things on earth are ignorant, so next comes Meng hexagram which is symbolic of ignorance.

(肖莉莉 译)

（二）《尚书》
Shangshu

1 【原文】柔远能迩，惇德允元，而难任人，蛮夷率服。

《尚书·商书·舜典》

【今译】安抚远民、爱护近臣，亲近品德高尚的人，信任心地善良的人，而又拒绝奸邪狡猾之徒，这样可使天下归心，四海臣服。

（张龑真 译）

【英译】Be kind to the distant, and cultivate the near. Give honour to the virtuous, and your confidence to the good, while you discountenance the artful—so shall the barbarous tribes lead on one another to make their submission.

（理雅各，2013）[17]

2 【原文】教胄子，直而温，宽而栗，刚而无虐，简而无傲。

《尚书·商书·舜典》

【今译】教导年轻人，为人应当正直温和，宽大而谨慎，性情刚毅而不盛气凌人，态度简约而不傲慢。

（张龑真 译）

【英译】To teach the young generation to be honest and gentle, generous and cautious, tough but not domineering, simple but not arrogant.

（张龑真 译）

3 【原文】克勤于邦，克俭于家，不自满假，惟汝贤。

《尚书·虞书·大禹谟》

【今译】治国要勤勉，持家要节俭，不自满、不自大，只有你最贤能。

（张龑真 译）

【英译】You should be diligent in running your country, thrifty in running your family, not complacent or arrogant, then you will be the most virtuous.

（张龑真 译）

4 【原文】满招损，谦受益，时乃天道。

《尚书·虞书·大禹谟》

【今译】自满的人会招来损害，谦虚的人会受到益处，这通常是自然规律。

（张龑真 译）

【英译】Haughtiness invites harm, modesty brings benefit, and this is the natural law.

（张龑真 译）

5 【原文】无稽之言勿听，弗询之谋勿庸。

《尚书·虞书·大禹谟》

【今译】未经查核证实的话不要听信，没有征询过意见的谋略不能轻用。

（张龑真 译）

【英译】Do not listen to what has not been checked and verified. Do not follow plans about which you have not sought counsel.

（张奭真 译）

6 【原文】惠迪吉，从逆凶，惟影响。

《尚书·虞书·大禹谟》

【今译】顺着道理做事就会吉祥如意，违逆道理做事就是凶灾。二者如影随形，似响应声。

（张奭真 译）

【英译】Accordance with the right leads to good fortune; disobeying the law leads to bad omen—just like shadows and echo.

（理雅各，2013）27

7 【原文】儆戒无虞，罔失法度。罔游于逸，罔淫于乐。
　　　　任贤勿贰，去邪勿疑。疑谋勿成，百志惟熙。

《尚书·虞书·大禹谟》

【今译】警惕戒备不要出差错，不要放弃法度，不要放纵地享受舒适安逸，不要无节制地玩乐。任用有贤能的人时不要怀疑，罢黜邪佞的人时不要犹豫。心存疑虑的谋划不要实行，各种思虑应当广阔。

（张奭真 译）

【英译】Admonish yourself to caution, when there seems to be no occasion for anxiety. Do not fail to observe the laws and ordinances. Do not find your enjoyment in idleness. Do not go to excess in pleasure. In your employment of men of worth, let none come between you and them. Put away evil without hesitation. Do not carry out plans, of (the wisdom of) which you have doubts. Study that all your purposes may be with the light of reason.

（理雅各，2013）27

8 【原文】慎厥身，修思永。惇叙九族，庶明励翼，迩可远，在兹。

《尚书·虞书·皋陶谟》

【今译】为人言行应当克己谨慎，自身的修养要坚持不懈。要使九族宽厚顺从，群哲勉力相佐。由近及远，先从自身做起。

（张奭真 译）

【英译】Let him be careful about his personal cultivation, with thoughts that are far-reaching, and thus he will produce a generous kindness and nice observance of distinctions among the nine branches of his kindred. All the intelligent (also) will exam themselves in his service; and in this way from what is near he will reach to what is distant.

（理雅各，2013）39

9 【原文】("九德")宽而栗，柔而立，愿而恭，乱而敬，扰而毅，直而温，简而廉，刚而塞，强而义。

《尚书·虞书·皋陶谟》

【今译】为人宽厚而又能庄严,处事柔和又有主见,待人随和而又恭敬,有才干而又认真,耐心随顺而又果敢坚定,正直而又温和,处事通达而又公正廉明,刚正而又笃实,坚强勇敢而又能遵守道义。

(张奚真 译)

【英译】A man of virtue should be generous yet solemn, tender yet strong-minded, easy-going yet respectful, capable yet earnest, patient and obedient yet resolute, righteous yet gentle, open-minded yet righteous, upright yet honest, brave yet moral.

(张奚真 译)

10 【原文】威克厥爱,允济;爱克厥威,允罔功。

《尚书·夏书·胤征》

【今译】威严胜过慈爱,就一定能成功;慈爱胜过权威,就不能成功。

(张奚真 译)

【英译】If majesty overcomes compassion, success will follow. When mercy overcomes authority, no merit can be achieved.

(张奚真 译)

11 【原文】慎厥终,惟其始。

《尚书·商书·仲虺之诰》

【今译】谨慎地对待事情的结局,在于谨慎对待它的开始。

(张奚真 译)

【英译】He who would take care of the end must be prudent with the beginning.

(张奚真 译)

12 【原文】天道福善祸淫。

《尚书·商书·汤诰》

【今译】上天之道会保佑善良的人,而给坏人降祸灾。

(张奚真 译)

【英译】God blesses the good and brings disaster to the bad.

(张奚真 译)

13 【原文】立爱惟亲,立敬惟长,始于家邦,终于四海。

《尚书·商书·伊训》

【今译】只要是亲人就应当关爱,只要是长辈就应当尊敬,这种做法开始于家庭,推及至国家,最终推广到天下。

(张奚真 译)

【英译】To set up love, you need to start with loving (your relations); to set up respect, you need to respect (your elders). The beginning is in the family and the state; the outcome is in (all within) the four seas.

(理雅各,2013)[103]

14 【原文】居上克明,为下克忠,与人不求备,检身若不及。

《尚书·商书·伊训》

【今译】处在上位能够明察下情,作为臣下能够竭诚尽忠;对待他人不求全责备,检点自身唯恐来不及。

(张奚真 译)

【英译】Occupying the highest position, he displayed intelligence; occupying an inferior position, he displayed his loyalty; he allowed (the good qualities of) the men (whom he employed), and did not seek that they should have every talent; in the government of himself, he seemed to think that he could never (sufficiently) attain.

(理雅各,2013)[105]

15 【原文】天作孽,犹可违;自作孽,不可逭。

《尚书·商书·太甲中》

【今译】上天降下的灾祸,还可以逃避;自己酿成的罪孽,无处可逃。

(张奚真 译)

【英译】The calamities of heaven may be avoided, but there is no escape from the iniquities of one's own making.

(张奚真 译)

16 【原文】奉先思孝,接下思恭。视远惟明,听德惟聪。

《尚书·商书·太甲中》

【今译】奉祀祖先应当纯孝,接待臣下应当谦恭。对于遥远的未来,眼睛要明察,听取有德之人的善言,耳朵要聪敏。

(张奚真 译)

【英译】In worshipping your ancestors, you should have filial piety; in reception of subordinates you should be humble and respectful. For the distant future, you should try to get clear views; it is wise to have your ears ever open to lessons of virtue.

(张奚真 译)

17 【原文】若升高,必自下,若陟遐,必自迩。

《尚书·商书·太甲下》

【今译】若想登高,须从低处开始,若要行远,须从脚下开始。

(张奚真 译)

【英译】If you want to climb high, you have to start from the bottom. If you want to go far, you have to begin from where it is near.

(张奚真 译)

18 【原文】有言逆于汝心,必求诸道;有言逊于汝志,必求诸非道。

《尚书·商书·太甲下》

【今译】有违背你心意的言论,一定要考虑它是否合乎道义;有投合你心意的话语,一定要考虑它的不合情理。

(张奚真 译)

【英译】When you hear something offensive, you have to ponder if it's right; when you hear something that accords with your point of views, you have to consider if it's contrary to what's right.

(张奚真 译)

19 【原文】若网在纲,有条而不紊;若农服田力穑,乃亦有秋。

《尚书·商书·盘庚》

【今译】犹如将网结在纲绳上一样,做事就有条理而不紊乱;犹如农夫在田间耕作一样,耗费了精力和力气,秋天才会有好收成。

(张奚真 译)

【英译】When the net has its line, there is order and not confusion; and when the husbandman labours upon his fields, he would have a good harvest in autumn only.

(张奚真 译)

20 【原文】有其善,丧厥善;矜其能,丧厥功。惟事事,乃其有备,有备无患。

《尚书·商书·说命中》

【今译】夸耀自己美好,就会失掉其美好;夸耀自己能干,就会失去其成功。做事情,就要有准备,有准备才没有后患。

(张奚真 译)

【英译】Boasting of one's merits, he may lose them; being vain of one's competence, he may not succeed; for all things, adequate preparation is a must to avert calamities.

21 【原文】无启宠纳侮,无耻过作非。

《尚书·商书·说命中》

【今译】不要宠幸奸邪而自取其辱,不要以改过为耻而铸成大错。

(张奚真 译)

【英译】Don't favor the wicked and treacherous and make a fool of yourself; don't make a blunder by being ashamed to admit mistakes.

(张奚真 译)

22 【原文】人求多闻,时惟建事,学于古训乃有获。事不师古,以克永世,匪说攸闻。惟学,逊志务时敏,厥修乃来。允怀于兹,道积于厥躬。惟教学半,念终始典于学,厥德修罔觉。

《尚书·商书·说命下》

【今译】人们寻求博学多识,这是想要建立事业。从古训当中学习才会有所收获。建立事业不吸取前人经验,还能维持长久的,没有听过有这种事。学习只有虚心谦逊,不懈努力,品德的完美自然就会实现。相信和记住这些,道德在自己身上将会积累增多。教与学是互相促进的,教人是学习的一半,持之以恒一心扑在学习上,道德会不知不觉地逐步完善。

(张奚真 译)

【英译】People seek rich knowledge and experience to make achievements. I have never heard of anyone who can attain the goal and be perpetuated for generations without learning from previous experience. As long as one learns with a humble and modest mind and unremitting efforts, moral perfection will be achieved naturally. Believe in and remember these, morality will accumulate day by day. Teaching and learning promote each other. Teaching is the half of learning. If we persevere in learning, morality will gradually grow unconsciously. If a man's thoughts are constantly fixed on learning, his virtuous cultivation would come unperceived.

(张奠真 译)

23 【原文】若金，用汝作砺；若济巨川，用汝作舟楫；若岁大旱，用汝作霖雨。启乃心，沃朕心，若药弗瞑眩，厥疾弗瘳；若跣弗视地，厥足用伤。

《尚书·商书·说命上》

【今译】(教师的作用)像是铁器，要用你做磨石；就像是渡大河，要用你做船和桨；又像是年岁大旱，要用你做霖雨。敞开你的心泉来灌溉我的心吧！比如药物不猛烈，疾病就不会好；比如赤脚而不看路，脚因此会受伤。

(张奠真 译)

【英译】A teacher is like a millstone for grinding iron; a teacher is like a boat and oar for crossing a river; And a teacher is like a rain in a drought. Open your heart to enlighten me! If the medicine is not strong, the disease will not be cured; if I am barefoot and don't look at the road, the foot will be injured.

(张奠真 译)

24 【原文】五事：一曰貌，二曰言，三曰视，四曰听，五曰思。貌曰恭，言曰从，视曰明，听曰聪，思曰睿。恭作肃，从作义，明作哲，聪作谋，睿作圣。

《尚书·周书·洪范》

【今译】一是容貌，二是言论，三是观察，四是听闻，五是思考。容貌要恭敬，言论要正当，观察要明白，听闻要广远，思考要通达。容貌恭敬就能严肃；言论正当就能治理；看问题清晰，就有智者风范；听闻广远就能善谋；思考通达就能圣明。

(周秉钧，2013)[188]

【英译】The following are the five (personal) matters. The first is the bodily demeanour; the second, speech; the third, seeing; the fourth, hearing; the fifth, thinking. (The virtue of) the bodily appearance is respectfulness; of speech, accordance (with reason); of seeing, clearness; of hearing, distinctness; of thinking, perspicaciousness. The respectfulness becomes manifest in gravity; accordance (with reason), in orderliness; the clearness, in wisdom; the distinctness, in deliberation; and the perspicaciousness, in sageness.

(理雅各，2013)[189]

25 【原文】德盛不狎侮。狎侮君子，罔以尽人心；狎侮小人，罔以尽其力。

《尚书·周书·旅獒》

【今译】品德高尚的人对待他人不会轻蔑戏辱。戏弄侮辱君子，就无法得到他的真心；戏弄侮辱百姓，就不可以使他们竭尽全力。

(张奠真 译)

【英译】A noble man will not humiliate others. If you tease and insult a gentleman, you can't get his sincerity; if you tease and insult common people, you can't make them do their best.

(张奠真 译)

26 【原文】玩人丧德,玩物丧志。志以道宁,言以道接。不作无益害有益,功乃成;不贵异物贱用物,民乃足。

《尚书·周书·旅獒》

【今译】戏弄人会丧失德行,玩弄物就丧失志向。立志要在正道上才能够安定;言论要合乎道义才可以接纳。不要做没有好处的事情来妨害有益的事,那么事情就可以成功;不以奇珍异宝为贵而看贱日用物资,百姓就能富足。

（张奠真 译）

【英译】Teasing people will ruin one's virtue, and finding amusement in things will ruin one's ambition. One's aims should repose in what is on the right path; one's speech is accepted when it's moral. Do not do anything that is not good to interfere with beneficial things, then his merit can be completed. Do not value rare and precious things over the necessities, so the people will have sufficient supplies.

（张奠真 译）

27 【原文】夙夜罔或不勤,不矜细行,终累大德。为山九仞,功亏一篑。

《尚书·周书·旅獒》

【今译】早晚如果不勤勉努力,不注重小节和作风,到头来会伤害大节。这犹如堆积一座九仞高的山,只因差最后一竹筐土而无法成功。

（张奠真 译）

【英译】Early and late never be but diligent. If we don't pay attention to the small actions, it will affect your virtue in great matters. It's like piling up a nine foot high mountain. We can't succeed even if we are short of the last basket of soil.

（张奠真 译）

28 【原文】功崇惟志,业广惟勤。惟克果断,乃罔后艰。

《尚书·周书·周官》

【今译】功高是由于有志向,业大是由于工作勤劳。只有办事果断的人,才没有后来的艰辛。

（张奠真 译）

【英译】Merit is due to the high aim, and an outstanding achievement is due to diligence. Only those who act decisively can avoid the future difficulties.

（张奠真 译）

29 【原文】作德,心逸日休;作伪,心劳日拙。

《尚书·周书·周官》

【今译】做善事,就会心气和平,而且一天天显示出美好;行欺诈,就会费尽心机,反而一天天显示出笨拙。

（张奠真 译）

【英译】Do good deeds, so that you will be peaceful, and become more admirable day by day. Practise them in hypocrisy, and your minds will be toiled, and you will show clumsiness day by day.

（张奠真 译）

30 【原文】不学墙面,莅事惟烦。

《尚书·周书·周官》

【今译】人如果不学习,就犹如面墙而立,一旦面临事情时,就会烦乱。

（张夔真 译）

【英译】Without study, it will be as if you're facing a wall, and you will be faced with a lot of trouble when you come across something.

（张夔真 译）

31 【原文】必有忍,其乃有济;有容,德乃大。

《尚书·周书·君陈》

【今译】一定要忍耐,事业才能成功;有包容万物的襟怀,德行才算伟大。

（张夔真 译）

【英译】Only by being patient can we succeed in our career, and only by having forbearance can we have great virtue.

（张夔真 译）

(三)《诗经》
The Book of Poetry

1 【原文】鹑之奔奔,鹊之彊彊。
　　　　人之无良,我以为兄!
　　　　鹊之彊彊,鹑之奔奔。
　　　　人之无良,我以为君!

《诗经·国风·鹑之奔奔》

【今译】鹌鹑双双共栖止,喜鹊对对齐飞翔。这人腐化又无耻,为何以他为兄长。喜鹊尚且成双对,鹌鹑也是双双飞。这人腐化又无耻,为何尊他为国君。

（肖莉莉 译）

【英译】The quails perch in couples;
　　　　The magpies fly in pairs.
　　　　Shameless is the man;
　　　　Whom I must call "brother".
　　　　The magpies dwell in twos;
　　　　The quails fly in company.
　　　　Shameless is the man;
　　　　Whom I must call "monarch".

（肖莉莉 译）

2 【原文】相鼠有皮,人而无仪。人而无仪,不死何为!

《诗经·国风·相鼠》

【今译】老鼠尚且还有毛皮,有人却不讲什么礼仪。一个人要是不讲礼仪,为何还不死去!

(肖莉莉 译)

【英译】Even a rat has its skin,
But a man may have no decency.
If he lacks decency,
What shall he do but die?

(肖莉莉 译)

3 【原文】有匪君子,如切如磋,如琢如磨。

《诗经·国风·淇奥》

【今译】文采斐斐的君子,(他的学问修养)就像那切磋过的象牙,就像那琢磨过的美玉。

(肖莉莉 译)

【英译】There is our elegant and refined Junzi(a man of virtue),
Like carved ivory,
And jade polished.

(肖莉莉 译)

4 【原文】投我以木桃,报之以琼瑶。

《诗经·国风·木瓜》

【今译】她拿木桃投赠我,我用美玉作回报。

(肖莉莉 译)

【英译】She presents a peach to me,
I give her a jade in return.

(肖莉莉 译)

5 【原文】它山之石,可以攻玉。

《诗经·小雅·鹤鸣》

【今译】别处山上的石头,亦可以用来琢磨玉器。

(肖莉莉 译)

【英译】Stones of other hills,
May be used to polish jades.

(肖莉莉 译)

6 【原文】高山仰止,景行行止。

《诗经·小雅·车辖》

【今译】(人品学问)德如高山人所仰慕,行若大道令人钦佩。

(肖莉莉 译)

【英译】People of lofty virtue deserve respect, as mountains of lofty height deserve up-look!

(肖莉莉 译)

7 【原文】靡不有初,鲜克有终。

《诗经·大雅·荡》

【今译】万事无不有开始,但很少有人能够善始善终。

（肖莉莉 译）

【英译】All things are commenced well, but few are concluded perfectly.

（肖莉莉 译）

（四）《左传》
Zuo Zhuan (Chronicle of Zuo)

1. 【原文】善不可失,恶不可长。

《左传·隐公六年》

【今译】善良不可丢失,邪恶不可助长。

（肖莉莉 译）

【英译】Goodness cannot be discarded, and evil cannot be developed.

（肖莉莉 译）

2. 【原文】人谁无过？过而能改,善莫大焉。

《左传·宣公二年》

【今译】哪个人会没有过错？有了过错能够改正,就再也没有比这更好的事情了。

（肖莉莉 译）

【英译】To err is human. It will be good if one can mend them.

（肖莉莉 译）

3. 【原文】太上有立德,其次有立功,其次有立言,虽久不废,此之谓三不朽。

《左传·襄公二十四年》

【今译】人生最首要的是"立德",即首重高尚之品德;其次是"立功",即建功立业;再次是"立言",即创立学说,提出有真知灼见的言论。此三者经久不废,不会磨灭,是谓"不朽"。

（肖莉莉 译）

【英译】Virtues can be the most important thing in one's life. Fostering achievements comes next. The third is to establish doctrines and put forward insightful comments. These three are combined in what is called "three eternities".

（肖莉莉 译）

4. 【原文】德,国家之基也。

《左传·襄公二十四年》

【今译】德行是国家的基础。

（肖莉莉 译）

【英译】Lofty virtue is the basis of a country.

（肖莉莉 译）

5. 【原文】私仇不及公,好不废过,恶不去善,义之经也。

《左传·哀公五年》

【今译】私人之间的怨仇不能影响到公事,喜爱一个人不能无视他的过错,厌恶一个人也不能抹杀他的优点,这是道义的根本。

(肖莉莉 译)

【英译】One cannot affect public affairs due to his own private enmity. One cannot ignore faults due to his own personal preference. One cannot cloak good behind bad due to his own individual disgust. These are the essential manifestation of righteousness.

(肖莉莉 译)

(五)《黄帝内经》
Huangdi Neijing (Inner Cannon of the Yellow Emperor)

1 【原文】精神内守,病安从来。

《素问·上古天真论篇第一》

【今译】精神内敛而不损耗,这样疾病怎么还会侵扰呢?

(肖莉莉 译)

【英译】If Jingshen (Essence-Spirit) remains inside without any loss, disease will find no way to occur.

(肖莉莉 译)

2 【原文】非其人勿教,非其真勿授,是谓得道。

《素问·金匮真言论篇第四》

【今译】对于那些并不具备一定资质或者并非真心实意有志于此的人,切勿轻易传授。这才是应有的态度。

(肖莉莉 译)

【英译】For those who are not qualified or possess no sincere desire to learn, do not teach without consideration. This is the right attitude.

(肖莉莉 译)

3 【原文】智者察同,愚者察异。

《素问·阴阳应象大论篇第五》

【今译】有智慧的人能够观察到客观规律的同一现象,而愚笨的人只观察到事物的不同的现象。

(肖莉莉 译)

【英译】A wise man is observant of common ground of things while a clumsy fool can only perceive difference.

(肖莉莉 译)

4 【原文】天之在我者德也,地之在我者气也。德流气薄而生者也。

《灵枢·本神第八》

【今译】天赋予我的是德,地赋予我的是气,天德地气阴阳相合,万物乃生。

(肖莉莉 译)

【英译】What the heaven has endowed me is De (natural law). What the earth has endowed me is Qi (basic materials). The integration of De(Yin) and Qi(Yang) brings out all things in the world.

(肖莉莉 译)

(六)《道德经》
Tao Te Ching

1 【原文】上善若水。

(《道德经》第八章)

【今译】至高的善行就像流水一样。

(肖莉莉 译)

【英译】The highest good is like water.

(肖莉莉 译)

2 【原文】持而盈之,不如其已。

(《道德经》第九章)

【今译】手中执持许多,已经到了盈满的状态,不如适可而止。

(肖莉莉 译)

【英译】One ought to stop in time rather than stretch a bow to the very full.

(肖莉莉 译)

3 【原文】宠辱若惊,贵大患若身。

(《道德经》第十三章)

【今译】得宠和受辱一样,都会使人惊慌、激动;重视这些灾祸就如同爱护自己的身体一样。

(肖莉莉 译)

【英译】Favor and disgrace are both disturbing, which should be weighed as one's body.

(肖莉莉 译)

4 【原文】夫唯不争,故天下莫能与之争。

(《道德经》第二十二章)

【今译】不与人争名争利,所以天下才没有人能和你相争。

(肖莉莉 译)

【英译】One who does not struggle for fame and fortune will find that no one under heaven can contend against him.

(肖莉莉 译)

5 【原文】自伐者无功;自矜者不长。

(《道德经》第二十四章)

【今译】自夸其功,反而无功;自骄尊大,反而难以长久。

（肖莉莉 译）

【英译】He who brags will gain no achievement; he who prides himself will not endure long.

（肖莉莉 译）

6 【原文】知人者智;自知者明。

（《道德经》第三十三章）

【今译】能洞察别人的人,可称之为有智慧的人;能洞察自己的人,可称之为明智的人。

（肖莉莉 译）

【英译】He who knows others is intelligent; He who knows himself is sensible.

（肖莉莉 译）

7 【原文】大巧若拙,大辩若讷。

（《道德经》第四十五章）

【今译】有智慧的却像是笨拙的,最雄辩的却像是木讷的。

（肖莉莉 译）

【英译】The greatest skill seems clumsy; the greatest eloquence seems tongue-tied.

（肖莉莉 译）

8 【原文】修之于身,其德乃真;修之于家,其德乃余;修之于乡,其德乃长;修之于邦,其德乃丰;修之于天下,其德乃普。

（《道德经》第五十四章）

【今译】一个人只有修身,他的德行才是真实的;如果他的家人和他一起修持,他的德行才绰绰有余;如果他能带领同乡人一起修持,他的德行才能够有所增长;如果他的修持能推广到整个国家,他的德行就会丰富起来;如果他的修持能推广到全天下,他的德行才能够更加普及。

（肖莉莉 译）

【英译】Cultivate morality in the individual, and its virtue will be genuine; cultivate morality in the family, and its virtue will be sufficient; cultivate morality in the village, and its virtue will grow; cultivate morality in the state, and its virtue will flourish; cultivate morality in the world, and its virtue will be pervasive.

（肖莉莉 译）

9 【原文】知者不言,言者不知。

（《道德经》第五十六章）

【今译】真正悟道的人并不多言,真正多言的人并不悟道。

（肖莉莉 译）

【英译】One who knows does not speak; one who speaks does not know.

（肖莉莉 译）

10 【原文】祸兮,福之所倚;福兮,祸之所伏。

（《道德经》第五十八章）

【今译】灾祸啊,福祉就倚伴在你的旁边;福祉啊,灾祸就潜伏在你之中。

(肖莉莉 译)

【英译】Behind every good fortune leans a bad fortune; behind every bad fortune lurks a good fortune.

(肖莉莉 译)

11 【原文】我有三宝,持而保之:一曰慈;二曰俭;三曰不敢为天下先。

(《道德经》第六十七章)

【今译】我有三件宝贝,一直收藏着它们:一是仁慈;二是节俭;三是谦让不争,不敢身居于天下人之前。

(肖莉莉 译)

【英译】I have three treasures which I hold and guard: The first and foremost is benevolence. The second one is frugality. The third is never to take the lead in the world.

(肖莉莉 译)

12 【原文】信言不美;美言不信。

(《道德经》第八十一章)

【今译】可信的话并不美丽;美丽的话并不可信。

(肖莉莉 译)

【英译】True words are not beautiful; beautiful words are not true.

(肖莉莉 译)

(七)《管子》
Guanzi

1 【原文】必得之事,不足赖也;必诺之言,不足信也。

《管子·形势》

【今译】肯定能办成的事情,不一定可靠;肯定能兑现的诺言,不值得相信。

(张燚真 译)

【英译】What is sure to be done is not reliable; what is sure to be fulfilled is not trustworthy.

(张燚真 译)

2 【原文】不为不可成,不求不可得。

《管子·牧民》

【今译】不去做不可能办到的事情,不去追求不可能得到的东西。

(张燚真 译)

【英译】Never pursue a goal which is unreachable; never seek something that is unattainable.

(张燚真 译)

3 【原文】仓廪实而知礼节,衣食足而知荣辱。

《管子·牧民》

【今译】百姓的粮仓充足、丰衣足食,才能顾及礼仪,重视荣誉和耻辱。

(张龚真 译)

【英译】Only when people have adequate food and clothes and their granaries are sufficient, can they have the sense of etiquette, honor and humility.

(张龚真 译)

4 【原文】成功立事,必顺于理义,故不理不胜天下,不义不胜人。

《管子·七法》

【今译】要想事业能成功,必须要顺应理义,所以不合于理就不能战胜天下,不合于义就不能战胜他人。

(张龚真 译)

【英译】Reason and justice are decisive in achieving success in career. One must comply with the principle and justice. Therefore, if one does not conform to the principle, one cannot conquer the world. By conforming to the principle, one can defeat others.

(张龚真 译)

5 【原文】宁过于君子,而毋失于小人。过于君子,其为怨浅;失于小人,其为祸深。

《管子·立政》

【今译】宁得罪君子,也不要得罪小人。对君子有过失,君子的怨气小,对小人犯了错,那自己就大祸临头了。

(张龚真 译)

【英译】Better offend a gentleman than a villain. It will only bring benign discontent if you have made a mistake with a gentleman. But with villain, you will be faced with imminent disaster.

(张龚真 译)

6 【原文】事者,生于虑,成于务,失于傲。

《管子·乘马》

【今译】做成一件事,往往产生于周密考虑,成功于实践探索,失败于骄傲自满。

(张龚真 译)

【英译】To accomplish a thing often results from careful consideration; success is the result of practical exploration, and failure is the result of haughtiness.

(张龚真 译)

7 【原文】规矩者,方圆之正也。虽有巧目利手,不如拙规矩之正方圆也。故巧者能生规矩,不能废规矩而正方圆也。

《管子·法法》

【今译】圆规、矩尺是校正方和圆的工具,你眼睛和手不管有多么巧妙和利索,也不如笨拙的圆规、矩尺来校正方形和圆形。所以能工巧匠可以制造出规和矩,却不能废除规和矩来正方定圆。

(张龚真 译)

【英译】No matter how skillful and agile your eyes and hands are, it's better to use a common compass and carpenters' square to rectify squares and circles. Although it is a skilled craftsman who makes a compass and a carpenter's square, he cannot rectify the circle and square without them.

（张奚真 译）

8 【原文】济于舟者，和于水矣。义于人者，祥其神矣。

《管子·白心》

【今译】水平静没有风浪，则能载舟；与人相处和睦，则神会保佑他福祥。

（张奚真 译）

【英译】Just as calm water can float a boat, a person at peace is blessed by God.

（张奚真 译）

9 【原文】目贵明，耳贵聪，心贵智。

《管子·九守》

【今译】眼睛贵在明辨事物，耳朵贵在听觉灵敏，心思贵在思维敏捷。

（张奚真 译）

【英译】Eyes are to see clearly, ears to hear sensibly and the mind to think wisely.

（张奚真 译）

10 【原文】少而习焉，其心安焉，不见异物而迁焉。

《管子·小匡》

【今译】人在年少时就开始学习，用心专一，心思安定，不会看见其他事物而分神。

（张奚真 译）

【英译】People who begin to learn at an early age are more likely to be attentive and stable. They will not be distracted by other things.

（张奚真 译）

11 【原文】审其所好恶，则其长短可知也；观其交游，则其贤不肖可察也。

《管子·权修》

【今译】仔细观察人们的喜好和厌恶，那么就可以了解他们的长处和不足；仔细观察人们交游的对象，就可以发现他们是否贤能。

（张奚真 译）

【英译】By observing people's likes and dislikes carefully, one can learn their merits and failings. One can find out whether people are virtuous or not by examining their friends carefully.

（张奚真 译）

12 【原文】天道之极，远者自亲；人事之起，近亲造怨。

《管子·形势》

【今译】奉行天道做事，疏远的人都会自然而然地亲近；开始计较个人之事，即使亲近的人也要生怨恨。

（张奚真 译）

【英译】People who are estranged will naturally get close to each other if they follow the way of heaven. Even intimates will hold a grudge against each other if the idea for pursuing the personal interests occurs to them.

（张燊真 译）

13 【原文】万物之于人也，无私近也，无私远也，巧者有余，而拙者不足。

《管子·形势》

【今译】天下的事物对于每个人来说都是公平的，不会亲近，也不会疏远，能巧妙利用的人会有富余，而对于笨拙的人来说永远也不够。

（张燊真 译）

【英译】Nothing in the world is in shortage or in abundance. People who can make good use of it will have plenty, but it will never be enough for those who are clumsy.

（张燊真 译）

14 【原文】小谨者不大立，訾食者不肥体。

《管子·形势》

【今译】眼光短浅拘于小节的人难有大的建树，这就好比厌食挑食的人身体不会健壮一样。

（张燊真 译）

【英译】People who are short-sighted can't make great achievements, as a man who is anorexic and picky cannot be healthy.

（张燊真 译）

15 【原文】孝弟者，仁之祖也。忠信者，交之庆也。

《管子·戒》

【今译】孝悌是仁的根本，忠信是交往的凭借。

（张燊真 译）

【英译】Filial piety is the foundation of benevolence, and faithfulness is the basis of communication.

（张燊真 译）

16 【原文】邪行亡乎体，违言不存口，静然定生，圣也。

《管子·戒》

【今译】身上没有邪僻的行为，口中没有悖理的言论，从而安定心性，这样的人就是圣人啊。

（张燊真 译）

【英译】The man with no improper deeds and unreasonable words is deemed a saint in that he is peaceful in mind.

（蔡希勤，2012）[165]

17 【原文】夫心有欲者，物过而目不见，声至而耳不闻也。

《管子·心术上》

【今译】心充满了嗜欲，万物在眼前却看不到，声音在耳畔也听不到。

（张燊真 译）

【英译】With a heart full of lust, nothing can be seen even it's in front of the eyes nothing can be heard, even the voice is around the ears.

（张奠宙 译）

18 【原文】一年之计，莫如树谷；十年之计，莫如树木；终身之计，莫如树人。

《管子·权修》

【今译】做一年的计划，不如种些稻谷；要做十年的计划，不如种植树木；要做终身的计划，不如培育人才。

（张奠宙 译）

【英译】To make a one-year plan, it's better to plant rice; to make a plan for a decade, it's better to plant trees; to make a lifelong plan, it is better to cultivate talents.

（张奠宙 译）

19 【原文】朝忘其事，夕失其功。邪气袭内，正色乃衰。

《管子·形势》

【今译】如果早上忘记了自己分内的事，那么到了晚上就会失去自己应有的功劳。不正之气侵入体内，健康的肤色就会衰退。

（张奠宙 译）

【英译】One who has accomplished nothing at the end of the day must not have worked hard during the day. A man will have a wretched appearance if he is evil and wicked inside.

（蔡希勤，薛彧威，2012）[187]

20 【原文】壮者无怠，老者无偷，顺天之道，必以善终者也。

《管子·中匡》

【今译】壮年的时候不懈怠，老年的时候不偷安，行事能够遵循天道，就一定能够得以善终。

（张奠宙 译）

【英译】Don't be lazy in one's prime, and don't drift along in one's old age. Follow these natural laws and one will live a full and peaceful life.

（张奠宙 译）

（八）《论语》
The Analects of Confucius

1 【原文】子曰："学而时习之，不亦说乎？有朋自远方来，不亦乐乎？人不知而不愠，不亦君子乎？"

《论语·学而》

【今译】孔子说："学习并且时常温习实践，这难道不是令人愉快的事情吗？有朋友从远方来访，难道不是让人高兴的事情吗？别人不了解或认可我，我也不心存怨恨，这难道不是君子所为吗？"

（肖莉莉 译）

【英译】Confucius remarks, "Isn't a pleasure to acquire knowledge and review it regularly? Isn't it a joy to have friends coming from afar? Isn't he a Junzi(a man of virtue) who will not be annoyed when others fail to recognize and appreciate him?"

（肖莉莉 译）

2 【原文】有子曰："其为人也孝弟,而好犯上者,鲜矣；不好犯上,而好作乱者,未之有也。君子务本,本立而道生。孝弟也者,其为仁之本与？"

《论语·学而》

【今译】有子说："一个人孝顺父母,敬重兄长,却又经常冒犯自己的长辈或上级,这样的人可以说非常少；不会对自己的长辈或上级不恭,却又经常犯上作乱,这样的人可说是从来就没有过。君子就该专心致力于道德的根本,根基建立了,治国做人之道也就有了。孝顺父母、敬重兄长,这就是'仁'的根本啊！"

（肖莉莉 译）

【英译】Youzi(a disciple of Confucius) says, "A man who has filial piety and fraternal love will seldom offend his superior; a man who does not offend his superior will never rebel. Junzi(a man of virtue) dedicates himself to fundamental issues, when the foundation is established, the 'Dao' of ruling the country and conducting oneself will naturally occur. Filial piety and fraternal love can be the root of benevolence！"

（肖莉莉 译）

3 【原文】曾子曰："吾日三省吾身：为人谋而不忠乎？与朋友交而不信乎？传不习乎？"

《论语·学而》

【今译】曾子说："我每天都会多次反省自身：帮别人谋划办事是否尽心竭力？与朋友交往是否诚实守信？老师传授的知识是否已经温习？"

（肖莉莉 译）

【英译】Zengzi(a disciple of Confucius) says, "I daily examine myself on three points：Have I stretched myself to work out plans for others? Have I been trustworthy when having social intercourse with friends? Have I failed to review what have been handed down to me？"

（肖莉莉 译）

4 【原文】子曰："弟子入则孝,出则悌,谨而信,泛爱众,而亲仁。行有余力,则以学文。"

《论语·学而》

【今译】孔子说："年轻人在家要孝敬父母,出门在外要敬爱兄长,为人处事谨言慎行,诚实守信,博爱众人,并且亲近有仁德的人。做到了这些还有余力,就可以继续学习典籍。"

（肖莉莉 译）

【英译】Confucius remarks, "A young man should honor his parents at home and respect his elders when out in the world. He should be cautious with his words and actions, be trustworthy in what he says, cherish all living beings, and should develop closer friendship with virtuous people. Then if he still has any energy to spare, he may set out to learn the classics."

（肖莉莉 译）

5 【原文】子夏曰："贤贤易色；事父母，能竭其力；事君，能致其身；与朋友交，言而有信。虽曰未学，吾必谓之学矣。"

《论语·学而》

【今译】子夏说："崇尚品德替代崇尚容貌；侍奉父母能够竭尽全力；服侍君主，能在必要的时候献出自己的生命；同朋友交往，能够言出必行恪守信用。这样的人，即便没有受过什么教育，我也认为他有学问。"

（肖莉莉 译）

【英译】Zixia (a disciple of Confucius) says, "A person who values virtue more than beauty, who goes all out serving his parents, who gives his life to the prince when necessary, and who is trustworthy when having social intercourse with friends can be an educated man even though he has not gotten any education."

（肖莉莉 译）

6 【原文】子曰："君子不重则不威；学则不固。主忠信。无友不如己者；过则勿惮改。"

《论语·学而》

【今译】孔子说："君子不庄重就不会有威严；即使读书，所学的东西也不牢固。恪守忠信，不交往品行不如自己的朋友；有了过错，不要怕改正。"

（肖莉莉 译）

【英译】Confucius remarks, "Junzi (a man of virtue) who lacks a dignified manner will not inspire stateliness. What he has learned will not remain permanent. Make it the guiding principle to adhere to righteousness and faithfulness. Do not make friends with the inferiors. Whenever you make a mistake, do not hesitate to correct it."

（肖莉莉 译）

7 【原文】子禽问于子贡曰："夫子至于是邦也，必闻其政，求之与，抑与之与？"子贡曰："夫子温、良、恭、俭、让以得之。夫子之求之也，其诸异乎人之求之与？"

《论语·学而》

【今译】子禽问子贡说："夫子（孔子）每到一个国家就总是能知道这个国家的政事，他是求人告诉他的呢，还是人家主动告诉他的呢？"子贡回答说："夫子具备和蔼、贤良、恭敬、俭朴、谦逊的品德，这是夫子求取的方法，大概与别人的方法不同吧！"

（肖莉莉 译）

【英译】Ziqin (a disciple of Confucius) once asked Zigong (another disciple of Confucius), "Whenever the Master comes into a country he is always informed of its government affairs. Does he seek for the information or is it given to him?" "Our Master gets it by being gracious, virtuous, respectful, thrifty and modest." replied Zigong, "The way our Master obtains information is quite different from ways of other people."

（肖莉莉 译）

8 【原文】有子曰:"信近于义,言可复也;恭近于礼,远耻辱也;因不失其亲,亦可宗也。"

《论语·学而》

【今译】有子说:"许下的诺言符合道义标准,这样才能信守诺言。态度的恭敬合于礼节,这样就能避免羞辱。依靠关系亲近的人,也就靠得住了。"

(肖莉莉 译)

【英译】Youzi(a disciple of Confucius)says, "When a promise is in line with moral standard, it can be fulfilled. When one's sincere attitude accords with etiquette, one may avoid humiliation. When one counts on close relationships, reliability is assured."

(肖莉莉 译)

9 【原文】子曰:"君子食无求饱,居无求安,敏于事而慎于言,就有道而正焉,可谓好学也已。"

《论语·学而》

【今译】孔子说:"君子不追求饮食的过分满足,不追求居住的安逸,做事敏捷而言谈谨慎,向有道德的人求教以匡正自己的缺点,就可以说是好学了。"

(肖莉莉 译)

【英译】Confucius remarks, "Junzi(a man of virtue) seeks neither an excessive appetite for food nor a comfortable home. He is quick in action but cautious in speech. He keeps company with virtuous people so as to put things right. Such a man can be described as eager to learn."

(肖莉莉 译)

10 【原文】子贡曰:"贫而无谄,富而无骄,何如?"子曰:"可也。未若贫而乐,富而好礼者也。"子贡曰:"《诗》云:'如切如磋!如琢如磨',其斯之谓与?"子曰:"赐也!始可与言《诗》已矣,告诸往而知来者。"

《论语·学而》

【今译】子贡说:"虽然贫穷却不谄媚奉承,富有却不骄纵自大,您认为这样的人怎么样?"孔子说:"这样的人也算是不错了。但比不上贫穷却能乐道,富有却能好礼的人。"子贡说:"就像《诗经》上说的,要像加工骨角、象牙、玉石一样,切磋它,琢磨它,这就是做人或做学问的方法吧?"孔子说:"子贡啊!可以开始和你讨论《诗经》了。告诉你已知的,就能从中推知未来的。"

(肖莉莉 译)

【英译】Zigong(a disciple of Confucius)says, "Though poor but not flattering, rich but not arrogant, What do you think of this kind of person?" Confucius replies, "This kind of person is not bad, but he is not as good as poor but contenting with poverty, wealthy but observant of the rites." Zigong says, "As said in *The Book of Poetry*, like bone has been cut, like jade has been polished, we must cut and file, we must chisel and grind. That is what you mean, isn't it?" Confucius says, "Ah! now I can begin to talk about *The Book of Poetry* with you. If I tell you the past, you can infer the future from it."

(肖莉莉 译)

11 【原文】子曰:"不患人之不己知,患不知人也。"

《论语·学而》

【今译】孔子说:"不要担心别人不了解自己,应当担心的是自己不了解别人。"

(肖莉莉 译)

【英译】Confucius remarks, "One should not worry about not to be understood by others; one should worry about not understanding others."

(肖莉莉 译)

12 【原文】子曰:"为政以德,譬如北辰,居其所而众星共之。"

《论语·为政》

【今译】孔子说:"如果国君以仁德来治理国政,自己就会像北极星一样,安居在自己的位置而其他星辰都环绕在它的周围。"

(肖莉莉 译)

【英译】Confucius remarks, "He who governs a country by means of morality, is just like the Pole-star, which keeps its place while all the other stars revolve round it."

(肖莉莉 译)

13 【原文】子曰:"《诗》三百,一言以蔽之,曰:'思无邪。'"

《论语·为政》

【今译】孔子说:"《诗经》三百篇,用一句话来概括就是:思想纯正。"

(肖莉莉 译)

【英译】Confucius remarks, "The theme that threads through the three hundred pieces in *The Book of Poetry* can be summed up in only one line: 'Let there be no evil thoughts.'"

(肖莉莉 译)

14 【原文】子曰:"道之以政,齐之以刑,民免而无耻;道之以德,齐之以礼,有耻且格。"

《论语·为政》

【今译】孔子说:"如果用政令来引导民众,用刑法来整顿民众,民众只会千方百计避免获罪,却没有廉耻之心;如果用道德教化民众,用礼制约束民众,民众不但有廉耻之心,而且人心归服。"

(肖莉莉 译)

【英译】Confucius remarks, "Guide the people by edicts, regulate them by penal law, and they will try to keep away from punishments without any sense of shame. Guide the people by morality, restrain them with rites, and they will not only have a sense of shame but also will order themselves."

(肖莉莉 译)

15 【原文】子曰:"吾十有五而志于学,三十而立,四十而不惑,五十而知天命,六十而耳顺,七十而从心所欲,不逾矩。"

《论语·为政》

【今译】孔子说:"我十五岁的时候立志于学习,三十岁时立身处世能站稳脚跟,说话做事都有把握,四十岁时因懂得了各种事情而不为外界事物困惑,五十岁我懂得顺应天道因循之理,六十岁听到别人说什么都可以明辨是非真假,对人和事都能豁达地容纳,七十岁则能行动都顺乎本心天性而又不会逾越规矩。"

(肖莉莉 译)

【英译】Confucius remarks, "At fifteen I set my heart on learning; at thirty I was sure of my way and gained a foothold; at forty I knew all kinds of things and no longer suffered from bewilderment; at fifty I got aware of the destiny; at sixty I could tell right from wrong and attune whatever I heard; at seventy I could follow my heart to do whatever I want without violating the rules."

(肖莉莉 译)

16 【原文】孟武伯问孝,子曰:"父母唯其疾之忧。"

《论语·为政》

【今译】孟武伯向孔子请教孝道。孔子说:"使父母只为子女的疾病担忧。"

(肖莉莉 译)

【英译】Meng Wubo asks about filial piety. Confucius answers, "Give your parents nothing to worry about other than illness."

(肖莉莉 译)

17 【原文】子夏问孝,子曰:"色难。"

《论语·为政》

【今译】子夏问孔子什么是"孝"。孔子说:"孝道就是很难做到始终对父母和颜悦色。"

(肖莉莉 译)

【英译】Zixia(a disciple of Confucius) asks about being filial. Confucius says, "It all lies in showing a kind and pleasant countenance on one's face all the time."

(肖莉莉 译)

18 【原文】子曰:"温故而知新,可以为师矣。"

《论语·为政》

【今译】孔子说:"在温习旧知识的过程中,能有新的心得体会,就可以当老师了。"

(肖莉莉 译)

【英译】Confucius remarks, "If a man will constantly go over what he has learned and keep adding something new to the old, he may become a teacher."

(肖莉莉 译)

19 【原文】子曰:"学而不思则罔,思而不学则殆。"

《论语·为政》

【今译】孔子说:"只读书而不思考,就会困惑迷惘;只思考而不读书,那就危险了。"

(肖莉莉 译)

【英译】Confucius remarks, "Learning without thinking will lead to perplexity; thinking without learning can be perilous."

(肖莉莉 译)

20 【原文】子曰:"由,诲汝知之乎?知之为知之,不知为不知,是知也。"

《论语·为政》

【今译】孔子说:"仲由!教给你对待知或者不知的态度吧,知道就是知道,不知道就是不知道,这就是智慧啊。"

(肖莉莉 译)

【英译】Confucius remarks, "You(a disciple of Confucius), shall I shed some light on this issue for you? To say you know when you really know, and to say you do not when you do not, this is wisdom."

(肖莉莉 译)

21 【原文】子曰:"人而无信,不知其可也。"

《论语·为政》

【今译】孔子说:"为人不讲信誉,不知他怎么可以立身处世。"

(肖莉莉 译)

【英译】Confucius remarks, "I do not know how men can get on in the world without any credit."

(肖莉莉 译)

22 【原文】子曰:"人而不仁,如礼何?人而不仁,如乐何?"

《论语·八佾》

【今译】孔子说:"一个人如果没有仁德,礼有什么用呢?为人不仁,乐有什么用呢?"

(肖莉莉 译)

【英译】Confucius remarks, "How can a man devoid of virtue practice rites! How can a man devoid of virtue practice music!"

(肖莉莉 译)

23 【原文】林放问礼之本。子曰:"大哉问!礼,与其奢也,宁俭;丧,与其易也,宁戚。"

《论语·八佾》

【今译】林放向孔子请教礼的根本。孔子回答说:"这个问题很重要!礼仪,与其奢侈不如俭朴;丧礼,与其仪式铺张不如内心真正悲戚。"

(肖莉莉 译)

【英译】Lin Fang (a disciple of Confucius) asks about the root of the rites. Confucius answers, "A big question indeed! With the rites, it is better to be frugal than to be extravagant; with funerals, heartfelt grief can be much better than grandiose rituals."

(肖莉莉 译)

24 【原文】子曰:"里仁为美,择不处仁,焉得知?"

《论语·里仁》

【今译】孔子说:"居住的地方有仁德之人才好,如果居住时不选择和贤德的人作邻居,怎么能说是明智的呢?"

(肖莉莉 译)

【英译】Confucius remarks, "It is nice to dwell among the virtuous. How can it be wise not to have such a choice?"

(肖莉莉 译)

25 【原文】子曰:"不仁者不可以久处约,不可以长处乐。仁者安仁,知者利仁。"

《论语·里仁》

【今译】孔子说:"没有仁德的人不能长久承受困窘,也不能长期经受安乐。仁者实行仁德以安身立命,智者施行仁德以谋取大利。"

(肖莉莉 译)

【英译】Confucius remarks, "A man without benevolence cannot endure hardship for long, nor can he long enjoy peace and happiness. The virtuous men take their stand in being moral; the wise men find it advantageous to be moral."

(肖莉莉 译)

26 【原文】子曰:"唯仁者能好人,能恶人。"

《论语·里仁》

【今译】孔子说:"只有具备了仁德的人才知道怎样去喜爱一个人,怎样去厌恶一个人。"

(肖莉莉 译)

【英译】Confucius remarks, "Only a man of virtue knows how to like people, and how to dislike them."

(肖莉莉 译)

27 【原文】子曰:"苟志于仁矣,无恶也。"

《论语·里仁》

【今译】孔子说:"如果一个人立志实行仁德,就不会有恶行了。"

(肖莉莉 译)

【英译】Confucius remarks, "If a man aims at benevolence, he will be free from evil."

(肖莉莉 译)

28 【原文】子曰:"朝闻道,夕死可矣。"

《论语·里仁》

【今译】孔子说:"如果早晨听闻了真理,即使当天晚上死去也没有什么遗憾了。"

(肖莉莉 译)

【英译】Confucius remarks, "If a man has learnt the truth in the morning, he may die willingly in the evening."

(肖莉莉 译)

29 【原文】子曰:"君子怀德,小人怀土;君子怀刑,小人怀惠。"

《论语·里仁》

【今译】孔子说:"君子心怀道德,小人安于乡土;君子关心法度,小人在意恩惠。"

(肖莉莉 译)

【英译】Confucius remarks, "While Junzi(a man of virtue) cherishes morality, the villain cherishes his native land. While the former expects laws, the latter expects favours."

(肖莉莉 译)

30 【原文】子曰:"君子喻于义,小人喻于利。"

《论语·里仁》

【今译】孔子说:"君子懂得的是道义,小人懂得的是利益。"

(肖莉莉 译)

【英译】Confucius remarks, "Junzi(a man of virtue) knows what is moral, while the villain knows what is profitable."

(肖莉莉 译)

31 【原文】子曰:"见贤思齐焉,见不贤而内自省也。"

《论语·里仁》

【今译】孔子说:"看到贤德的人,就应该向他学习、看齐。见到缺少贤德的人,就应该自我反省有没有和他一样的缺点毛病。"

(肖莉莉 译)

【英译】Confucius remarks, "When you see a man of virtue, think whether you equal him; when you see a man devoid of virtue, look inward and examine yourself."

(肖莉莉 译)

32 【原文】子曰:"父母在,不远游,游必有方。"

《论语·里仁》

【今译】孔子说:"父母在世,子女不宜到远方游历。如果要出远门,也一定要有确定的去处。"

(肖莉莉 译)

【英译】Confucius remarks, "While your parents are alive, you should not go far. If you really do, your whereabouts should always be known."

(肖莉莉 译)

33 【原文】子曰:"君子欲讷于言而敏于行。"

《论语·里仁》

【今译】孔子说:"君子要言谈审慎,行动敏捷。"

(肖莉莉 译)

【英译】Confucius remarks, "Junzi(a man of virtue) should be slow in speech but quick in action."

(肖莉莉 译)

34 【原文】子曰:"德不孤,必有邻。"

《论语·里仁》

【今译】孔子说:"有道德的人是不会孤单的,一定会有志同道合人与他同行。"

(肖莉莉 译)

【英译】Confucius remarks, "A man of virtue will never be alone. He is sure to have neighbors."

(肖莉莉 译)

35 【原文】子曰:"朽木不可雕也,粪土之墙不可杇也!"

《论语·公冶长》

【今译】孔子说:"腐烂的木头无法雕刻,粪土筑起的墙壁不能粉刷。"

(肖莉莉 译)

【英译】Confucius remarks, "One cannot carve anything out of rotten wood nor trowel a wall of dung and dirt. "

(肖莉莉 译)

36 【原文】子曰:"敏而好学,不耻下问。"

《论语·公冶长》

【今译】孔子说:"他聪明勤勉而且好学,而且不以向地位低于自己的人请教为耻。"

(肖莉莉 译)

【英译】Confucius remarks, "He was quick and eager to learn, and was not ashamed to ask his inferiors. "

(肖莉莉 译)

37 【原文】季文子三思而后行。子闻之,曰:"再,斯可矣。"

《论语·公冶长》

【今译】季文子每做一件事都要考虑多次。孔子听到后说:"考虑两次也就足够了。"

(肖莉莉 译)

【英译】Ji Wenzi always thought three times before acting. On hearing of this, Confucius remarks, "Twice is enough. "

(肖莉莉 译)

38 【原文】吾闻之也:"君子周急不济富。"

《论语·雍也》

【今译】我听说过:"君子只救济那些急需的人,而不是救济富有的人。"

(肖莉莉 译)

【英译】I have heard it said, "Junzi(a man of virtue) is ready to help the needy instead of the rich. "

(肖莉莉 译)

39 【原文】子曰:"质胜文则野,文胜质则史。文质彬彬,然后君子。"

《论语·雍也》

【今译】孔子说:"质朴胜于文采,就会显得粗野;文采胜过质朴,就又未免虚浮。只有质朴和文采结合适当,才能成为君子。"

(肖莉莉 译)

【英译】Confucius remarks, "When a man's plainness overwhelms refinement, he tends to be rough; conversely, when a man's refinement overwhelms plainness, he tends to be superficial. A combination of the two results in gentlemanliness. "

(肖莉莉 译)

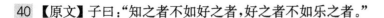

40 【原文】子曰:"知之者不如好之者,好之者不如乐之者。"

《论语·雍也》

【今译】孔子说:"对于任何事物,了解它的人比不上喜爱它的人,喜爱它的人比不上以此为乐的人。"

(肖莉莉 译)

【英译】Confucius remarks, "Those who love it are better than those who merely know it; those who take pleasure in it are better than those who merely love it."

(肖莉莉 译)

41 【原文】子曰:"知者乐水,仁者乐山;知者动,仁者静;知者乐,仁者寿。"

《论语·雍也》

【今译】孔子说:"有智慧的人喜欢水,有仁德的人喜欢山。有智慧的人活跃,有仁德的人沉静。有智慧的人快乐,有仁德的人长寿。"

(肖莉莉 译)

【英译】Confucius remarks, "The wise take delight in water; the benevolent take delight in mountains. The wise keep active; the benevolent stay still. The wise are cheerful; the benevolent are long-lived."

(肖莉莉 译)

42 【原文】子曰:"默而识之,学而不厌,诲人不倦,何有于我哉?"

《论语·述而》

【今译】孔子说:"默默地将(所见所闻)记在心里,努力学习而不感到厌烦,教导他人而不知道疲倦,这些事情我做到了哪些呢?"

(肖莉莉 译)

【英译】Confucius remarks, "Quietly keeping all the sights and sounds in mind, learning without boredom and instructing others without fatigue—what have I accomplished with these things?"

(肖莉莉 译)

43 【原文】子曰:"不愤不启,不悱不发。举一隅不以三隅反,则不复也。"

《论语·述而》

【今译】孔子说:"教导学生.不到他苦思冥想而仍然领会不了的时候,不去开导他;不到他想说却说不清楚的时候,不去启发他。教给他一个方面的知识,他却不能由此而推知其他三个方面的知识,那我就不再教他了。"

(肖莉莉 译)

【英译】Confucius remarks, "I never instruct anyone who are not driven with eagerness, and I never enlighten anyone who has not made things clear with weariness. When I help a man round one corner, if he does not get round the other three, I will not continue the lesson."

(肖莉莉 译)

44 【原文】子曰:"我非生而知之者,好古,敏以求之者也。"

《论语·述而》

【今译】孔子说:"我并不是生来就有知识的人,只是爱好古代文化,勤奋勉力地去求得知识的人。"

(肖莉莉 译)

【英译】Confucius remarks, "I was not born with knowledge but, being fond of ancient cultures, I am diligent in exploring it."

(肖莉莉 译)

45 【原文】子曰:"三人行,必有我师焉。择其善者而从之,其不善者而改之。"

《论语·述而》

【今译】孔子说:"几个人同行,其中必定有我可以取法学习做我老师的人。选择他们的长处去学习,将他们不足的地方作为借鉴而改正。"

(肖莉莉 译)

【英译】Confucius remarks, "Whenever I walk in the company of two others, I am bound to learn from one of them. Identifying their merits, I copy them, and identifying their demerits, I amend them accordingly."

(肖莉莉 译)

46 【原文】子曰:"君子坦荡荡,小人长戚戚。"

《论语·述而》

【今译】孔子说:"君子心怀坦荡,小人经常忧愁。"

(肖莉莉 译)

【英译】Confucius remarks, "Junzi(a man of virtue) is composed and at ease; while a villain is always full of worries."

(肖莉莉 译)

47 【原文】曾子有疾,孟敬子问之。曾子言曰:"鸟之将死,其鸣也哀;人之将死,其言也善。"

《论语·泰伯》

【今译】曾子病了,孟敬子去探望他。曾子对他说:"鸟将要死去的时候,它的叫声是悲哀的;人快要死的时候,他说的话是善意的。"

(肖莉莉 译)

【英译】Zengzi(a disciple of Confucius)was seriously ill. He said to a young noble of the court, Meng Jingzi who came to see him,"When a bird is dying, its song is sad; when a man is dying, his words are kind."

(肖莉莉 译)

48 【原文】曾子曰:"士不可以不弘毅,任重而道远。仁以为己任,不亦重乎?死而后已,不亦远乎?"

《论语·泰伯》

【今译】曾子说:"读书人不可以不刚强而有毅力,因为他们责任重大而道路遥远。以施行仁德于天下为自己的责任,难道还不重大吗?奋斗终生,到死方休,这个历程难道不遥远吗?"

(肖莉莉 译)

【英译】Zengzi(a disciple of Confucius) says, "A scholar must be resolute and unbending, for his burden is heavy and he has a long way to go. He takes carrying out benevolence as his duty. Is that not a heavy one? Only with death does his journey come to an end. Is the way not a long one?"

（肖莉莉 译）

49 【原文】子曰："不在其位，不谋其政。"

《论语·泰伯》

【今译】孔子说："不在那个职位上，就不要去考虑处在那个职位才会做的事情。"

（肖莉莉 译）

【英译】Confucius remarks, "One who holds no rank in a state should not concern himself with politics."

（肖莉莉 译）

50 【原文】子曰："学如不及，犹恐失之。"

《论语·泰伯》

【今译】孔子说："学习知识就像追赶什么东西似的，唯恐赶不上，赶上了，还会担心学到了又丢掉。"

（肖莉莉 译）

【英译】Confucius remarks, "Learn as if you were chasing something that you could not catch up, and as though you were frightened of losing it again."

（肖莉莉 译）

51 【原文】子曰："三军可夺帅也，匹夫不可夺志也。"

《论语·子罕》

【今译】孔子说："一国的军队，可以夺去它的主帅；一个男子汉，却不可以夺去他的志向。"

（肖莉莉 译）

【英译】Confucius remarks, "Even can the armies be deprived of their commander, can't still a man be deprived of his ambition."

（肖莉莉 译）

52 【原文】子曰："知者不惑，仁者不忧，勇者不惧。"

《论语·子罕》

【今译】孔子说："聪明的人不会疑惑，仁德的人不会忧愁，勇敢的人无所畏惧。"

（肖莉莉 译）

【英译】Confucius remarks, "Men of wisdom are free from doubts, men of benevolence are free from worries, and men of courage are free from fear."

（肖莉莉 译）

53 【原文】古之学者为己，今之学者为人。

《论语·宪问》

【今译】古代的人学习是为了提高自己的修养和学问，而现在的人学习是为了装饰自己给别人看。

（肖莉莉 译）

【英译】Confucius remarks, "Men in old days educated themselves to improve themselves; men today educate themselves to impress others."

（肖莉莉 译）

54 【原文】有教无类。

《论语·卫灵公》

【今译】人人都可以接受教育，没有贫富、贵贱、智愚、地域等等的区别。

（肖莉莉 译）

【英译】Education aims for all regardless of the learners' background.

（肖莉莉 译）

（九）《墨子》
Mozi

1 【原文】良弓难张，然可以及高入深；良马难乘，然可以任重致远；良才难令，然可以致君见尊。

《墨子·亲士第一》

【今译】好的弓难以拉开，但是能射得高、扎得深；好马难以驾驭，但是它可以负重行远；贤良的人才难以驱使，但是能够使国君更加受人尊敬。

（张冀真 译）

【英译】Good bows are hard to draw, but they can reach higher and pierce deeper. Good horses are hard to ride, but they can carry heavier loads and go farther. Talented people are hard to command, but they can make the lord more respected.

（张冀真 译）

2 【原文】江河不恶小谷之满己也，故能大。圣人者，事无辞也，物无违也，故能为天下器。

《墨子·亲士第一》

【今译】江河不嫌弃溪水灌注，才能汇成巨流。圣人不推辞难事，不违背事理，所以能成为治理天下的英才。

（张冀真 译）

【英译】Only when rivers don't despise the streams can they merge into mighty currents. Sages can be pillars in governing the world as they don't refuse difficult things or violate the principle.

（张冀真 译）

3 【原文】志不强者智不达，言不信者行不果。

《墨子·修身第二》

【今译】意志不坚强的人，智慧一定不高；说话不讲信用的人，行动一定不果敢。

（张冀真 译）

【英译】It's hard for a person with a weak will to have high intelligence; it's hard for a person who doesn't keep his promise to act decisively.

（张燧真 译）

4 【原文】君子之道也，贫则见廉，富则见义，生则见爱，死则见哀。

《墨子·修身第二》

【今译】君子处事的原则应当做到：贫穷的时候表现他的廉洁，富足的时候显示他的义气，活着的时候被人爱戴，去世的时候被人哀悼。

（张燧真 译）

【英译】A gentleman should be honest in poverty, generous in wealth. He is loved when he is alive, and mourned when he dies.

（张燧真 译）

5 【原文】爱人利人者，天必福之；恶人贼人者，天必祸之。

《墨子·法仪第四》

【今译】爱戴别人并且有利于他人的，天一定会赐福于他；仇视并且残害别人的，天一定会降祸于他。

（张燧真 译）

【英译】Heaven will surely bless those who love and benefit others, and bring disaster to those who hate and harm others.

（张燧真 译）

6 【原文】俭节则昌，淫佚则亡。

《墨子·辞过第六》

【今译】生活节俭，国家就会昌盛；骄奢放纵，国家就会衰亡。

（张燧真 译）

【英译】Moderation and frugality can bring prosperity, while indulgence and excess can only lead to destruction.

（张燧真 译）

7 【原文】有力者疾以助人，有财者勉以分人，有道者劝以教人。

《墨子·尚贤下第十》

【今译】有力气的人在帮助别人的时候行动迅速，有财富的人在散发钱财时倾尽全力，有高尚道德的人在教诲别人的时候讲明事理。

（张燧真 译）

【英译】People with strength act quickly when they help others; people with wealth do their best when they distribute money, and people with morality make sense when they teach others.

（张燧真 译）

8 【原文】天下兼相爱则治，交相恶则乱。

《墨子·兼爱上第十四》

【今译】天下人能彼此相亲相爱才会太平，互相仇恨就会动乱。

（张燧真 译）

【英译】Universal love will bring peace and order while mutual hatred will only lead to chaos to the world.

（张婓真 译）

9 【原文】仁人之事者，必务求兴天下之利，除天下之害。

《墨子·兼爱下第十六》

【今译】仁人做事，必须讲求对天下有利，为天下除害。

（张婓真 译）

【英译】Those who are benevolent in human affairs must strive for the benefit of the world and eliminate the harm of the world.

（张婓真 译）

10 【原文】天下有义则治，无义则乱。

《墨子·天志下第二十八》

【今译】天下有了道义就能安定，没有道义就会祸乱。

（张婓真 译）

【英译】The world will be governed if there is justice, the world will fall into chaos if there is no justice.

（张婓真 译）

11 【原文】利人乎，即为；不利人乎，即止。

《墨子·非乐上第三十二》

【今译】有利于别人的，就做下去；不利于别人的，就停止不做。

（张婓真 译）

【英译】Do what is beneficial to others, and reject what is harmful to others.

（张婓真 译）

12 【原文】今天下之士君子，忠实欲天下之富而恶其贫，欲天下之治而恶其乱，执有命者之言，不可不非，此天下之大害也。

《墨子·非命上第三十五》

【今译】现在天下的士人君子，内心着实希望天下富足而怕贫困，想使天下得到治理而厌恶动乱，那么就不能不反对那些主张有命的人所说的话，因为这是天下的大害啊！

（张婓真 译）

【英译】Nowadays, the elite gentlemen really hope that the world is rich and free from poverty, and that the country will govern without chaos. Then they must oppose what fatalism advocates say, because fatalism is a great harm to the world!

（张婓真 译）

13 【原文】为，穷知而县于欲也。

《墨子·经上第四十》

【今译】错误的行为，是穷于理智而又被欲望牵制而造成的。

（张婓真 译）

【英译】Wrong behavior is caused by being irrational and being restrained by desire.

（张婓真 译）

14 【原文】智少而不学,必寡。

《墨子·经说下第四十三》

【今译】如果知识少又不努力学习,必然会孤陋寡闻。

(张奠真 译)

【英译】People who have little knowledge and don't study hard are bound to be ignorant.

(张奠真 译)

15 【原文】智而不教,功适息。

《墨子·经说下第四十三》

【今译】有知识有智慧但是却不教授别人,功劳就停止了。

(张奠真 译)

【英译】If one has knowledge and wisdom but doesn't teach others, no credit will come to him/her.

(张奠真 译)

16 【原文】诸圣人所先,为人欲名实。名实不必名。

《墨子·大取第四十四》

【今译】众多圣人们的当务之急是要考核名与实,人应当要名实相符。但是有名不一定有实,有实不一定有名。

(张奠真 译)

【英译】The first thing saints would do is to straighten out the relationship between their names and reality. A man should live up to his name. However, The name does not necessarily match the reality.

(张奠真 译)

17 【原文】言足以复行者,常之;不足以举行者,勿常。不足以举行而常之,是荡口也。

《墨子·耕柱第四十六》

【今译】说的话能够办到,那就不妨常说;说的话不能办到,就不要总是讲。若是做不到还总是说,那就徒费口舌了。

(张奠真 译)

【英译】Words that can be put into action should be spoken frequently, otherwise they shouldn't be talked about very often. To speak frequently about what cannot be put into action is a waste of breath.

(张奠真 译)

18 【原文】嘿则思,言则诲,动则事,使三者代御,必为圣人。

《墨子·贵义第四十七》

【今译】静默的时候能思考,说话的时候能引导他人,行动的时候能办成事,如果这三者能交替运用,必定能成为一个圣人。

(张奠真 译)

【英译】When you are silent, you can think deeply; when you speak, you can guide others; when you act, you can accomplish things. If you can use these three alternately, you will be a saint.

（张奭真 译）

19 【原文】夫义,天下之大器也,何以视人,必强为之?

《墨子·公孟第四十八》

【今译】大义,是天下最可贵的东西,为什么一定要看他人行事,而不努力去做呢?

（张奭真 译）

【英译】Righteousness is the most valuable thing in the world. Why do we have to see others act instead of trying to do it ourselves?

（张奭真 译）

20 【原文】今施人薄而望人厚,则人唯恐其有赐于己也。

《墨子·鲁问第四十九》

【今译】如果现在送给别人薄礼,却希望得到人家丰厚的报答,那么人们就会怕你再送东西给他们了。

（张奭真 译）

【英译】If you give people a petty favor today, but hope to get rich rewards later, then people will be afraid that you will provide them something again.

（张奭真 译）

（十）《孟子》
Mencius

1 【原文】古之人与民偕乐,故能乐也。

《孟子·梁惠王上》

【今译】古代的君王能够与百姓同喜同乐,所以他自己也能得到真正的快乐。

（肖莉莉 译）

【英译】The monarchs of antiquity shared their pleasures with the people, and could thus get real happiness.

（肖莉莉 译）

2 【原文】仁者无敌。

《孟子·梁惠王上》

【今译】施行仁政的人是无敌于天下的。

（肖莉莉 译）

【英译】A benevolent ruler finds no opponents in the world.

（肖莉莉 译）

3 【原文】老吾老,以及人之老;幼吾幼,以及人之幼。

《孟子·梁惠王上》

【今译】尊敬自己的长辈,从而延及尊敬别人的长辈;爱护自己的儿女,从而延及爱护别人的儿女。

(肖莉莉 译)

【英译】Honor your own elders and extend it to those of others; love your own children and extend it to those of others.

(肖莉莉 译)

4 【原文】权,然后知轻重;度,然后知长短。

《孟子·梁惠王上》

【今译】称一称,方知轻重;量一量,才知长短。

(肖莉莉 译)

【英译】Only by weighing a thing, can you know whether it is light or heavy; and only by measuring it, can you know whether it is long or short.

(肖莉莉 译)

5 【原文】缘木求鱼,虽不得鱼,无后灾。

《孟子·梁惠王上》

【今译】爬上树去捉鱼,即便捉不到鱼,也不会有什么灾祸。

(肖莉莉 译)

【英译】No disaster follows if you climb a tree for fish but in vain.

(肖莉莉 译)

6 【原文】谨庠序之教,申之以孝悌之义,颁白者不负戴于道路矣。

《孟子·梁惠王上》

【今译】办好各类学校,用孝顺父母、尊敬兄长的道理反复教导学生,那么须发斑白的人就不会在路上负重行走了。

(肖莉莉 译)

【英译】If due concern is given to the running of schools, and stress is laid on the filial piety and fraternal affection repeatedly, the grey-haired people will not carry loads on the roads any more.

(肖莉莉 译)

7 【原文】曰:"独乐乐,与人乐乐,孰乐?"曰:"不若与人。"曰:"与少乐乐,与众乐乐,孰乐?"曰:"不若与众。"

《孟子·梁惠王下》

【今译】孟子说:"一个人独自欣赏音乐快乐,跟别人一起欣赏音乐也快乐,究竟哪一种更快乐些呢?"齐王说:"当然跟别人一起欣赏音乐更快乐些。"

孟子说:"跟少数人欣赏音乐快乐,跟多数人欣赏音乐也快乐,究竟哪一种更快乐呢?"齐王说:"当然跟多数人一起欣赏音乐更快乐。"

(肖莉莉 译)

【英译】Mencius asks, "Which is more delightful —to enjoy music by yourself alone, or to enjoy it with others?" "Along with others." "Which is more pleasant —to enjoy music with a few, or to enjoy it with many?" "To enjoy it with many."

（肖莉莉 译）

8 【原文】乐民之乐者,民亦乐其乐;忧民之忧者,民亦忧其忧。

《孟子·梁惠王下》

【今译】国君以百姓的快乐为自己的快乐,百姓也会以国君的快乐为自己的快乐;国君视百姓的忧愁为自己的忧愁,百姓也会视国君的忧愁为自己的忧愁。

（肖莉莉 译）

【英译】When a monarch delights in the joy of his people, his people will in turn delight in his joy; when a monarch grieves at the sorrow of his people, his people will naturally grieve at his sorrow.

（肖莉莉 译）

9 【原文】子贡曰:"学不厌,智也;教不倦,仁也。"

《孟子·公孙丑上》

【今译】子贡说"学习不满足,是一种智慧;教学不倦怠,是一种仁德"。

（肖莉莉 译）

【英译】Zigong says, "Learning without satiety is a kind of wisdom; teaching without weariness is a kind of benevolence."

（肖莉莉 译）

10 【原文】恻隐之心,仁之端也;羞恶之心,义之端也;辞让之心,礼之端也;是非之心,智之端也。

《孟子·公孙丑上》

【今译】同情之心是仁的开端,羞耻之心是义的开端,谦让之心是礼的开端,是非之心是智慧的开端。

（肖莉莉 译）

【英译】Compassion is the beginning of benevolence; shame is the beginning of righteousness; modesty is the beginning of propriety; and a distinction between right and wrong is the beginning of wisdom.

（肖莉莉 译）

11 【原文】天时不如地利,地利不如人和。

《孟子·公孙丑下》

【今译】有利的时机和气候不如有利的险阻、坚固的城池,有利的险阻、坚固的城池也不如得民心之和。

（肖莉莉 译）

【英译】Good timing is not as important as the favorable topographical situation, and the favorable topographical situation is not as important as the the union of people who are of the same mind.

（肖莉莉 译）

12 【原文】得道者多助,失道者寡助。

《孟子·公孙丑下》

【今译】施行仁政信守道义的人,帮助他的人就多;不行仁政丧失道义的人,帮助他的人就少。

(肖莉莉 译)

【英译】One who applies a policy of benevolence has many to support him, and one who denies a policy of benevolence has few to support him.

(肖莉莉 译)

13 【原文】劳心者治人,劳力者治于人。

《孟子·滕文公上》

【今译】脑力劳动者统治别人,体力劳动者被他人统治。

(肖莉莉 译)

【英译】Those who toil with their minds govern others; and those who labour with their muscles are governed by others.

(肖莉莉 译)

14 【原文】父子有亲,君臣有义,夫妇有别,长幼有叙,朋友有信。

《孟子·滕文公上》

【今译】父子之间要有骨肉之亲,君臣之间要有礼法之义,夫妻之间要有内外之别,长幼之间要有尊卑之序,朋友之间要有诚信之德。

(肖莉莉 译)

【英译】There should be affection between father and son, righteousness between monarch and minister, distinction between husband and wife, orderly sequence between old and young, and fidelity between friends.

(肖莉莉 译)

15 【原文】富贵不能淫,贫贱不能移,威武不能屈,此之谓大丈夫。

《孟子·滕文公下》

【今译】富贵不能让我骄奢淫逸,贫贱不能让我动摇意志,权势武力不能让我牺牲节操,这样才叫作大丈夫。

(肖莉莉 译)

【英译】All these characteristics contribute to a great man: wealth and rank never tempt him; poverty and obscurity never deflect him; power and force never subdue him.

(肖莉莉 译)

16 【原文】入则孝,出则悌,守先王之道,以待后之学者。

《孟子·滕文公下》

【今译】在家孝顺父母,在外尊敬长辈;奉行先王的礼法道义,并用来培养后代的学者。

(肖莉莉 译)

【英译】One is expected to be filial to his parents at home and be respectful to his elders abroad, adhering to the principles of the ancient kings and cultivating the future learners.

（肖莉莉 译）

17 【原文】天下之本在国，国之本在家，家之本在身。

《孟子·离娄上》

【今译】天下的根本在于国，国的根本在于家，而家的根本则是个人。

（肖莉莉 译）

【英译】The root of the world is in the state, the root of the state is in the family, and the root of the family is in the individual.

（肖莉莉 译）

18 【原文】顺天者存，逆天者亡。

《孟子·离娄上》

【今译】顺应时势的生存，违背时势的灭亡。

（肖莉莉 译）

【英译】Those who accord with Heaven live; those who defy Heaven perish.

（肖莉莉 译）

19 【原文】恭者不侮人，俭者不夺人。

《孟子·离娄上》

【今译】谦恭的人不会侮辱别人，节俭的人不会掠夺别人。

（肖莉莉 译）

【英译】A respectable man does not insult others; a thrifty man does not plunder others.

（肖莉莉 译）

20 【原文】人之患在好为人师。

《孟子·离娄上》

【今译】人的毛病，就在于喜欢在别人面前当老师。

（肖莉莉 译）

【英译】The trouble with people is that they are eager to be teachers of others.

（肖莉莉 译）

21 【原文】仁者爱人，有礼者敬人。

《孟子·离娄下》

【今译】有仁德的人爱护他人，有礼貌的人尊敬他人。

（肖莉莉 译）

【英译】A man of benevolence loves others; a man with good manners respects others.

（肖莉莉 译）

22 【原文】爱人者，人恒爱之；敬人者，人恒敬之。

《孟子·离娄下》

【今译】爱护别人的人,别人也会常常爱他;尊敬别人的人,别人也常常尊敬他。

（肖莉莉 译）

【英译】He who loves others will always be loved by others; he who respects others will always be respected by others.

（肖莉莉 译）

23 【原文】父母爱之,喜而不忘;父母恶之,劳而不怨。

《孟子·万章上》

【今译】父母喜爱自己,虽然高兴但却不能忘记自己做儿子的责任;父母讨厌自己,虽然忧愁,却不因此怨恨父母。

（肖莉莉 译）

【英译】One should not forget his duty as a son though he is glad that his parents love him; one should not feel agonizing and complain even though his parents dislike him.

（肖莉莉 译）

24 【原文】伯夷,目不视恶色,耳不听恶声。

《孟子·万章下》

【今译】伯夷这个人,眼睛不去看不好的事物,耳朵不去听不好的声音。

（肖莉莉 译）

【英译】Boyi turns a blind eye to vicious sights and a deaf ear to vicious sounds.

（肖莉莉 译）

25 【原文】天之生斯民也,使先知觉后知,使先觉觉后觉。

《孟子·万章下》

【今译】上天生育这些民众,就是要使先明理的人启发后明理的人,使先觉悟的人启发后觉悟的人。

（肖莉莉 译）

【英译】When Heaven begats the people, the man who are first informed should awaken those who have not, and the man who first apprehend should enlighten those who have not.

（肖莉莉 译）

26 【原文】鱼,我所欲也,熊掌,亦我所欲也;二者不可得兼,舍鱼而取熊掌者也。生,亦我所欲也;义,亦我所欲也;二者不可得兼,舍生而取义者也。

《孟子·告子上》

【今译】鱼是我想要的,熊掌也是我想要的;如果两者不能兼得,那我就舍弃鱼而要熊掌。生命是我想要的,道义也是我想要的;如果两者不能兼得,我宁肯舍弃生命而取道义。

（肖莉莉 译）

【英译】Fish is what I want, and bear's paw is also what I want; if I can not have both, I will prefer bear's paw to fish. Life is what I desire, and righteousness is also what I desire; if I can not have both, I will prefer righteousness to my life.

（肖莉莉 译）

27 【原文】故天将降大任于是人也,必先苦其心志,劳其筋骨,饿其体肤,空乏其身,行拂乱其所为,所以动心忍性,曾益其所不能。

《孟子·告子下》

【今译】所以上天要让某个人担负重任,必定先要让他的心志受苦,让他的筋骨劳累,让他的身体忍饥挨饿,让他备受穷困之苦,使他的每一行为总是不能如意。这样,便可以磨砺他的意志,坚韧他的性情,增长他的才干。

(肖莉莉 译)

【英译】Thus, when Heaven is about to place great responsibility upon a man, it will first temper his heart and mind with sufferings, fatigue his muscles and bones, starve his limbs and flesh, subject him to poverty and frustration, thwart and confound all his attempts, hence in this way his will is stirred up, his disposition hardened, and his competence strengthened.

(肖莉莉 译)

28 【原文】人恒过,然后能改;困于心,衡于虑,而后作;征于色,发于声,而后喻。

《孟子·告子下》

【今译】人总是经常犯错误,然后才能改正错误;心灵被困,思虑阻塞,然后才能奋发有所作为;表现在脸上,用语言表达出来,然后才能让人明白。

(肖莉莉 译)

【英译】A man inevitably makes mistakes, but he grows only when he amends his mistakes. In the same way, only when one is distressed in mind and perplexed in their thoughts will he give rise to reformation. Only when his feelings and thoughts are shown in his looks and expressed in words can he be understood.

(肖莉莉 译)

29 【原文】入则无法家拂士,出则无敌国外患者,国恒亡。然后知生于忧患而死于安乐也。

《孟子·告子下》

【今译】一个国家,如果在内没有守法度的臣民和辅弼的贤士,在外没有敌对的邻国和外来的忧患,常常容易灭亡。这样才能知道忧患的环境足以使人生存,安乐的环境足以使人败亡的道理了。

(肖莉莉 译)

【英译】If a state has no law-abiding subjects and wise counselors at home, and no hostile threats, sufferings and hardships abroad, it will perish easily. Then we will come to know that one survives in sufferings and hardships, and perishes in ease and comfort.

(肖莉莉 译)

30 【原文】穷则独善其身,达则兼善天下。

《孟子·尽心上》

【今译】窘困时便独自修养自己的身心,显达时便使天下之人都受到好处。

(肖莉莉 译)

【英译】when one is in adversity, he will attend to his own virtue in solitude; when one is in prosperity, he will strive to benefit the whole world.

（肖莉莉 译）

31 【原文】亲亲而仁民,仁民而爱物。

《孟子·尽心上》

【今译】君子应先亲爱自己的亲人,进而仁爱百姓;由仁爱百姓,进而爱惜万物。

（肖莉莉 译）

【英译】Junzi(a man of virtue) is affectionate to his parents and relatives, so he is benevolent to the people generally. He is benevolent to the people, so he treasures creatures in the world.

（肖莉莉 译）

32 【原文】养心莫善于寡欲。

《孟子·尽心下》

【今译】修养心性的方法莫过于减少物欲。

（肖莉莉 译）

【英译】For nurturing the mind, there is nothing better than to have few desires.

（肖莉莉 译）

33 【原文】孟子曰:"民为贵,社稷次之,君为轻。"

《孟子·尽心下》

【今译】孟子说:"百姓最为重要,国家在其次,君主最不重要。"

（肖莉莉 译）

【英译】Mencius said, "the people rank highest, next comes the country, and the sovereign matters least."

（肖莉莉 译）

（十一）《庄子》
Zhuangzi

1 【原文】小知不及大知,小年不及大年。

《庄子·逍遥游》

【今译】小聪明赶不上大智慧,寿命短的比不上寿命长的。

（肖莉莉 译）

【英译】Small knowledge does not parallel to the great nor a short life to a long one.

（肖莉莉 译）

2 【原文】至人无己,神人无功,圣人无名。

《庄子·逍遥游》

【今译】道德修养高尚的"至人"能够达到无一己私念的境界,精神世界超脱物外的

"神人"没有功名利禄的束缚,思想修养臻于完美的"圣人"没有名声地位的羁绊。

(肖莉莉 译)

【英译】A perfect man has no self; a spiritual man cares for no accomplishments; a sage pursues no fame.

(肖莉莉 译)

3 【原文】道隐于小成,言隐于荣华。

《庄子·齐物论》

【今译】大道被小的成就所掩盖,言论被浮华的辞藻所隐蔽。

(肖莉莉 译)

【英译】Dao is concealed by small achievements; speech is obscured by flowery words.

(肖莉莉 译)

4 【原文】可乎可,不可乎不可。道行之而成,物谓之而然。

《庄子·齐物论》

【今译】世上让人肯定的事物才让人认可,不能让人肯定的事物不能让人认可。道路是人们走出来的,事物的称谓是人们叫出来的。

(肖莉莉 译)

【英译】The possible is possible. The impossible is impossible. A road is made by thousand times of treading; a thing is so because it is called so.

(肖莉莉 译)

5 【原文】夫大道不称,大辩不言,大仁不仁,大廉不嗛,大勇不忮。

《庄子·齐物论》

【今译】至高无上的道不必称扬,最了不起的辩说不用言说,真正的仁爱不用向人表示仁爱,真正的廉洁不必向人表示谦让,真正的勇敢从不攻击他人。

(肖莉莉 译)

【英译】Great Dao is ineffable, great disputation does not require words, great benevolence is not purposely charitable, great honesty is not purposely modest, and great bravery is not aggressive.

(肖莉莉 译)

6 【原文】故知止其所不知,至矣。

《庄子·齐物论》

【今译】因此懂得知识的探索停止于自己所不知晓的境域,那就是极点了。

(肖莉莉 译)

【英译】Hence one who knows to stop at what he does not know has attained the ultimate.

(肖莉莉 译)

7 【原文】吾生也有涯,而知也无涯。以有涯随无涯,殆已;已而为知者,殆而已矣。

《庄子·养生主》

【今译】我们的生命是有限的,而知识却是无限的。以有限的生命去追求无限的知识,势必劳乏伤神。既然如此还要不停地追求知识,那可真是更加倦怠了。

（肖莉莉 译）

【英译】Our lives are limited, but knowledge is boundless. To pursue the unlimited with the limited can be weary. When knowing this, if one still goes after knowledge, One's life will be more weary.

（肖莉莉 译）

8 【原文】灾人者,人必反灾之。

《庄子·人间世》

【今译】加害别人的人一定会被别人所害。

（肖莉莉 译）

【英译】Those who hurt others will definitely be hurt by others in return.

（肖莉莉 译）

9 【原文】人皆知有用之用,而莫知无用之用也。

《庄子·人间世》

【今译】人们都知道有用的用处,却无人知道无用的用处。

（肖莉莉 译）

【英译】Everyone knows the utility of the useful, but nobody knows the utility of the useless.

（肖莉莉 译）

10 【原文】故德有所长,而形有所忘。

《庄子·德充符》

【今译】所以只要有过人的德行,形体方面的缺陷就会被人们遗忘。

（肖莉莉 译）

【英译】Thus, when one has outstanding virtue, his physical defects will be forgotten.

（肖莉莉 译）

11 【原文】知天之所为,知人之所为者,至矣。

《庄子·大宗师》

【今译】知道自然的作为,并且知道人的作为,这就是智慧的最高境界了。

（肖莉莉 译）

【英译】To know the work of nature and to know the work of man is the ultimate of wisdom.

（肖莉莉 译）

12 【原文】不忘其所始,不求其所终。受而喜之,忘而复之,是之谓不以心捐道,不以人助天。

《庄子·大宗师》

【今译】不忘记自己的本原,也不寻求自己的归宿,什么际遇都能欣然接受,忘掉生死像是自己复归自然,这就叫作不用心智去损害大道,也不用人为的因素去助力自然。

（肖莉莉 译）

【英译】The sage neither forget what his beginning has been nor seek what his end will be. He accepts with delight anything that comes to him, and forgets anything that he has forgotten. This is what is meant by not impairing Dao with the mind and not assisting the heaven with human efforts.

（肖莉莉 译）

13 【原文】同则无好也，化则无常也，而果其贤乎！

《庄子·德充符》

【今译】与万物同一就没有偏好，顺应变化就不执滞常理，你果真是贤人啊！

（肖莉莉 译）

【英译】Those who have become one with the infinite will have no preferences. Those who adapt to changes will have no more constants. Then you will be a real sage.

（肖莉莉 译）

14 【原文】彼至正者，不失其性命之情。

《庄子·骈拇》

【今译】所谓的至理正道，就是不偏离自然所赋予的事物的本性。

（肖莉莉 译）

【英译】He who adheres to rightness will not deviate from the original characteristics of his inborn nature.

（肖莉莉 译）

15 【原文】天下莫不以物易其性矣。小人则以身殉利，士则以身殉名，大夫则以身殉家，圣人则以身殉天下。

《庄子·骈拇》

【今译】天下没有谁不用外物而改变自身的本性。小人为了私利而牺牲自己，士为了名声而牺牲自己，大夫为了家族而牺牲自己，圣人则为了天下而牺牲自己。

（肖莉莉 译）

【英译】Throughout history everyone in the world has altered his inborn nature for the sake of something. The ordinary person sacrifices himself for the sake of personal gains; the nobleman sacrifices himself for the sake of fame; the high official sacrifices himself for the sake of his family; the sage sacrifices himself for the sake of the whole world.

（肖莉莉 译）

16 【原文】唇竭而齿寒。

《庄子·胠箧》

【今译】嘴唇没了牙齿便觉寒冷。

（肖莉莉 译）

【英译】When the lips are gone, the teeth will get cold.

（肖莉莉 译）

17 【原文】大巧若拙。

《庄子·胠箧》

【今译】最大的智巧看起来却显笨拙。

（肖莉莉 译）

【英译】The greatest wisdom looks clumsy.

（肖莉莉 译）

18 【原文】通于天地者，德也；行于万物者，道也；上治人者，事也；能有所艺者，技也。

《庄子·天地》

【今译】通达于天地的是"德"；周行于万物的是"道"；善于治理天下的是各任其事；能够让才能充分发挥的是各种技巧。

（肖莉莉 译）

【英译】Therefore, it is virtue that pervades heaven and earth; it is Dao that acts upon myriad things in the world; what makes the state well governed is administrative affairs; what lends art to ability is skill.

（肖莉莉 译）

19 【原文】故执德之谓纪，德成之谓立，循于道之谓备，不以物挫志之谓完。

《庄子·天地》

【今译】所以执守德行就是把握了万物的纲纪，德行的实践就称之为有建树，顺应大道就叫做完备，不因外物而损害心志就叫作德行完美。

（肖莉莉 译）

【英译】Therefore, to hold fast to virtue is called the guideline; to mature in virtue is called establishment; to follow Dao is called completion; not to allow things to distract the will is called perfection.

（肖莉莉 译）

20 【原文】不利货财，不近富贵；不乐寿，不哀夭；不荣通，不丑穷。

《庄子·天地》

【今译】不贪图财货，不追求富贵，不以长寿为快乐，不以夭折为悲哀，不把显达看作荣耀，不把穷困视为羞耻。

（肖莉莉 译）

【英译】He neither profits from goods or property nor associates with glory and wealth. He finds no joy in longevity, no grief in death, no honor in success, and no shame in poverty.

（肖莉莉 译）

21 【原文】德人者，居无思，行无虑，不藏是非美恶。四海之内共利之之谓悦，共给之之谓安。

《庄子·天地》

【今译】有德行的人居处时没有思索，行动时没有谋划，不计较是非美丑。与天下人共同分享利益就感到喜悦，共同分享财货便是安乐。

（肖莉莉 译）

【英译】The man of virtue dwells without thought and acts without plan. He has no concern for right and wrong, good and evil. He finds joy in sharing profit with all things within the four seas and peace in looking after the needs of others.

（肖莉莉 译）

22 【原文】大惑者，终身不解；大愚者，终身不灵。

《庄子·天地》

【今译】最迷惑的人,终身也不会醒悟;最愚昧的人,终身也不会明白。

(肖莉莉 译)

【英译】He who is in the worst confusion will never get straightened out for his entire life; he who is the worst fool will end his life without realizing it for his whole life.

(肖莉莉 译)

23 【原文】泉涸,鱼相与处于陆,相呴以湿,相濡以沫,不如相忘于江湖。

《庄子·天运》

【今译】泉水干涸了,鱼儿困在陆地上相互依偎,相互嘘吸湿气,用口沫相互湿润,倒不如在江湖里彼此相忘。

(肖莉莉 译)

【英译】When the springs dry up, the fish are left stranded on the land, spewing each other with moisture and damping each other with spit. But it would be much better if they could forget each other in the rivers and lakes!

(肖莉莉 译)

24 【原文】井蛙不可以语于海者,拘于虚也;夏虫不可以语于冰者,笃于时也;曲士不可以语于道者,束于教也。

《庄子·秋水》

【今译】井里的青蛙,不可能跟它谈论大海,这是因为地域的局限;夏天的虫子,不可能跟它谈论冰霜,这是因为受到时间的限制;乡下的书生,不可以和他谈论大道理,这是因为他受了礼教的束缚。

(肖莉莉 译)

【英译】You cannot talk about the sea with a frog at the bottom of a well for it is stuck in a small space, ice with a summer insect for it is confined by the season, and Dao with a scholar of distorted views for he is shackled by his doctrines.

(肖莉莉 译)

25 【原文】故大知观于远近。

《庄子·秋水》

【今译】所以具有大智慧的人无论远近都观照得到。

(肖莉莉 译)

【英译】Hence great wisdom observes both far and near.

(肖莉莉 译)

26 【原文】且子独不闻夫寿陵余子之学行于邯郸与?未得国能,又失其故行矣,直匍匐而归耳。

《庄子·秋水》

【今译】你没有听说过寿陵少年到邯郸学走路的事吗?他不但没学到赵国人走路的技巧,反而忘了自己走路的步法,结果只好爬着回去。

(肖莉莉 译)

【英译】Haven't you heard of the young boy from Shouling who tried to learn to walk the way people do in Handan? He failed to acquire this new skill and forgot his own way of walking. So all he could do was to crawl all the way back home.

(肖莉莉 译)

27 【原文】君子之交淡若水,小人之交甘若醴。君子淡以亲,小人甘以绝。

《庄子·山木》

【今译】君子之间的交情像水一样淡薄,小人之间的交情像甜酒一样甘美。君子之间的交情虽然淡薄但是亲切,小人之间的交情虽然甘甜却容易断绝。

(肖莉莉 译)

【英译】The relationship between Junzi(a man of virtue) is as insipid as water, while that between villains is as sweet as wine. The insipid relationship between Junzi (a man of virtue) gives rise to affection, while the sweet relationship between villains leads to disaffection.

(肖莉莉 译)

28 【原文】入其俗,从其令。

《庄子·山木》

【今译】到一个地方就要遵从那里的风俗习惯。

(肖莉莉 译)

【英译】Whenever you go to a new place, follow its customs and rules.

(肖莉莉 译)

29 【原文】夫知者不言,言者不知,故圣人行不言之教。

《庄子·知北游》

【今译】知道的人不说,说的人并不知道,所以圣人施行的是不靠说教的教导。

(肖莉莉 译)

【英译】Those who know do not speak; those who speak do not know. Therefore, the sage instructs without words.

(肖莉莉 译)

30 【原文】博之不必知,辩之不必慧。

《庄子·知北游》

【今译】学问广博的人不一定具有真知,善于辩论的人不一定具有慧见。

(肖莉莉 译)

【英译】Erudition does not necessarily mean real knowledge; eloquence does not necessarily imply wisdom.

(肖莉莉 译)

31 【原文】鸟兽不厌高,鱼鳖不厌深。夫全其形生之人,藏其身也,不厌深渺而已矣。

《庄子·庚桑楚》

【今译】鸟兽不厌高飞,鱼鳖不厌水深。那些保全身体的人要敛藏自己,也是不厌深远远罢了。

(肖莉莉 译)

【英译】Therefore, birds and beasts do not detest how high the mountain is; fish and turtles do not detest how deep the water is. Those who want to preserve their body and conceal themselves do not mind how remote or secluded they live.

(肖莉莉 译)

32 【原文】行乎无名者,唯庸有光。

《庄子·庚桑楚》

【今译】行事不拘名迹的人,即使平庸亦有光辉。

(肖莉莉 译)

【英译】He who does deeds without bringing any fame may be plain but brilliant.

(肖莉莉 译)

33 【原文】不能容人者无亲,无亲者尽人。

《庄子·庚桑楚》

【今译】不能容人的人无人亲近,无人亲近的人也就弃绝于人。

(肖莉莉 译)

【英译】He who can find no room for others will have no friends close to him. He who has no friends close to him will be strangers to others.

(肖莉莉 译)

34 【原文】以德分人谓之圣,以财分人谓之贤。

《庄子·徐无鬼》

【今译】能用德行去感化他人的人可称之为圣人,能用财物去周济他人的人可称之为贤人。

(肖莉莉 译)

【英译】He who shares his integrity with others is called a sage; he who shares his property with others is called a worthy.

(肖莉莉 译)

35 【原文】是故丘山积卑而为高,江河合水而为大,大人合并而为公。

《庄子·则阳》

【今译】所以山丘聚积卑小的石块才成就其高,江河汇聚细流才成就其大,伟人集思广益才成就其公。

(肖莉莉 译)

【英译】Thus mountains reach loftiness when small stones pile up; rivers achieve magnitude when small streams converge; the great men attain achievements when the others' traits accumulate.

(肖莉莉 译)

36 【原文】真者,精诚之至也。不精不诚,不能动人。

《庄子·渔父》

【今译】本真是精诚的极点。没有精诚就不能感动人。

(肖莉莉 译)

【英译】One's true nature is the acme of pure sincerity. Without sincerity and pureness, one cannot move others.

(肖莉莉 译)

37 【原文】君子不为苛察。

《庄子·天下》

【今译】君子不对他人吹毛求疵,求全责备。

(肖莉莉 译)

【英译】Junzi(a man of virtue) never demands perfection of others.

(肖莉莉 译)

(十二)《荀子》
Xunzi

1 【原文】君子曰:学不可以已。青,取之于蓝,而青于蓝;冰,水为之,而寒于水。木直中绳,輮以为轮,其曲中规,虽有槁暴,不复挺者,輮使之然也。故木受绳则直,金就砺则利,君子博学而日参省乎己,则知明而行无过矣。

《荀子·劝学》

【今译】君子说:"学习是不可以停止的。靛青是从蓼蓝中提炼出来的,但是它比蓼蓝更青;冰,是水冻结而成的,但是要比水寒冷得多。木料笔直而且合乎墨线的要求,但把它熏烤弯曲蹂制成车轮,却弯曲得和圆规相适应,以后即使烘烤暴晒,也不再变得挺直,这是熏烤弯曲使它变成这样的。所以木料在墨线的规范下就会笔直,金属制成的刀剑经过磨砺才能锋利,君子学识渊博而又能每天省察自己,那就会见识高明而行为没有过错了。"

(肖莉莉 译)

【英译】Junzi(a man of virtue) says:"Learning never comes to an end. Blue dye stems from the indigo plant, but it is bluer than the plant. Ice comes from water, but it is colder than water. Straight as a plumbline, wood can be made into a curved wheel which conforms to the compass by means of steaming and bending. It will not return to its former straightness even under the baking sun due to the process of steaming and bending. Likewise, wood becomes straight when marked with the plumbline, and metal becomes sharp when grinded on a whetstone. Junzi(a man of virtue) dabbles in everything and examines himself daily so that he will be learned and faultless."

(肖莉莉 译)

2 【原文】故不登高山,不知天之高也;不临深溪,不知地之厚也。不闻先王之遗言,不知学问之大也。

《荀子·劝学》

【今译】所以不登上高山,就不知道天空的高远;不俯视深不可测的山谷,就不知道大地的厚重;没有听到古代先王的遗言,就不知道学问的博大。

(肖莉莉 译)

【英译】If you do not climb a high mountain, you will never know the height of the sky. If you do not visit a deep ravine, you will never know the profoundness of the earth. If you have not heard the last words of the ancient kings, you will never know the magnificence of learning.

(肖莉莉 译)

3 【原文】神莫大于化道,福莫长于无祸。

《荀子·劝学》

【今译】没有比融于圣贤的道德更高的精神修养了,没有比无灾无难更大的幸福了。

(肖莉莉 译)

【英译】There's no better self-cultivation than being assimilated into the morality of sages; and there's no more blessing than being devoid of misfortune.

(肖莉莉 译)

4 【原文】吾尝终日而思矣,不如须臾之所学也;吾尝跂而望矣,不如登高之博见也。

《荀子·劝学》

【今译】我曾经整日地思索,但不如学习片刻收获得多;我曾经踮起脚跟向远方瞭望,但不如登上高处视野广阔。

(肖莉莉 译)

【英译】I once spent a whole day pondering, but it was not worthy of a moment's learning. I once stood on my tiptoes for an outlook, but it was not so amazing as the broad view from a high place.

(肖莉莉 译)

5 【原文】蓬生麻中,不扶而直;白沙在涅,与之俱黑。

《荀子·劝学》

【今译】蓬草生长在大麻当中,不用扶助也会长得挺直;雪白的沙子混在黑土中,就会变得和黑土一样黑。

(肖莉莉 译)

【英译】When conyza canadensis grows among hemp plants, they grow up straight without any support; when white sand is mixed up with black soil, it will become entirely black.

(肖莉莉 译)

6 【原文】君子居必择乡,游必就士,所以防邪辟而近中正也。

《荀子·劝学》

【今译】君子居住时必须选择乡邻,外出交游时必须接近贤士,这样是防止误入歧途而接近正道的方法。

(肖莉莉 译)

【英译】Junzi(a man of virtue) is sure to select carefully the place where he dwells, and he is sure to associate with men of virtue when he travels. This is how he prevents himself from going astray and approaches what is correct.

(肖莉莉 译)

7 【原文】故言有召祸也,行有召辱也,君子慎其所立乎!

《荀子·劝学》

【今译】所以言辞有时会招致灾祸,行动有时会招致耻辱,君子要小心自己的立身处事啊!

(肖莉莉 译)

【英译】Hence there are words that summon disaster, and there is conduct that incurs humiliation, so Junzi(a man of virtue) should be careful about where he takes his stand.

(肖莉莉 译)

8 【原文】积土成山,风雨兴焉;积水成渊,蛟龙生焉;积善成德,而神明自得,圣心备焉。故不积跬步,无以至千里;不积小流,无以成江海。骐骥一跃,不能十步;驽马十驾,功在不舍。锲而舍之,朽木不折;锲而不舍,金石可镂。

《荀子·劝学》

【今译】泥土积聚成了高山,风雨就会在那里兴起;水积聚成为深渊,蛟龙就会在那里生长;积累善行成了有道德的人,人就会变得聪明睿智,而圣人的思想境界也就具备了。所以不积累起一步两步,就无法到达千里之外;不汇集涓涓细流,就不能成为江海。骏马一跃,不会超过十步;劣马跑十天也能跑完千里的路程,因为它从不间断。雕刻东西,刻了一会儿就放下了,朽木也不能刻断;不停地刻镂下去,那么金石也能刻透。

(肖莉莉 译)

【英译】When earth piles up into mountains, wind and rain will arise from it. When water accumulates into a deep pool, dragons will be born within it. When goodness accumulates into virtue, a divine clarity of power will be naturally attained and a sagelike mind will occur. Without accumulating tiny paces, you will never reach a thousand li. Without accumulating small streams, you have no way to form river or sea. Even a fine horse cannot cover ten paces in a single leap. Even a worn-out nag can go far if it does not give up. If you start carving but give up, you will not be able to cut even rotten wood; but if you start carving and never give up, even metal and stone can be engraved.

(肖莉莉 译)

9 【原文】君子之学也,入乎耳,著乎心,布乎四体,形乎动静;端而言,蠕而动,一可以为法则。

《荀子·劝学》

【今译】君子对待学习的态度是:听在耳中,记在心中,表露在身体的仪态上,显现在行动举止中;所以轻声地说话,小心地行动,都可以成为别人效法的榜样。

(肖莉莉 译)

【英译】The learning of Junzi(a man of virtue) enters through his ears, goes deep to his heart, spreads through his four limbs, and manifests in his actions. His slight word, his subtle movement, all can serve as a model for others.

(肖莉莉 译)

10 【原文】故礼恭,而后可与言道之方;辞顺,而后可与言道之理;色从,而后可与言道之致。

《荀子·劝学》

【今译】所以请教的人恭敬有礼,然后才可以和他谈论道的法则;只有对方说话谦虚亲切,然后才可以和他谈论道的内容;他的表情谦逊和蔼,然后才可以和他谈论道的最高境界。

(肖莉莉 译)

【英译】Only if they are courteous and reverent can you talk about the methods of Dao(Confucian doctrines) with them. Only if their speech is amiable can you talk about the reasonableness of Dao(Confucian doctrines) with them. Only if their countenance is agreeable can you talk about the profoundness of Dao(Confucian doctrines) with them.

(肖莉莉 译)

11 【原文】君子崇人之德,扬人之美,非谄谀也;正义直指,举人之过,非毁疵也。

《荀子·不苟》

【今译】君子推崇别人的美德,褒扬别人的优点,不是谄媚阿谀别人;义正言辞地指出别人的缺点,揭露别人的过错,并不是故意诋毁别人的瑕疵。

(肖莉莉 译)

【英译】When Junzi(a man of virtue) venerates others' morality and publicize others' merits, it is not flattering. When he points out others' faults straightly, it is not slandering deliberately.

(肖莉莉 译)

12 【原文】君子洁其身而同焉者合矣;善其言而类焉者应矣。

《荀子·不苟》

【今译】君子洁修自身,志同道合的人就来聚合;修好自己的言论,同类的人就会来呼应。

(肖莉莉 译)

【英译】If Junzi(a man of virtue) cultivates his moral character, people of the same mind will accord with him. If Junzi(a man of virtue) refines his speech, people of the same kind will come to echo.

(肖莉莉 译)

13 【原文】材性知能,君子小人一也。好荣恶辱,好利恶害,是君子小人之所同也,若其所以求之之道则异矣。

《荀子·荣辱》

【今译】才性和智能,君子和小人是一样的。爱好荣誉、憎恶耻辱,喜好物利、厌恶祸害,这也是君子和小人相同的地方,但是他们求取的方式却大不相同。

(肖莉莉 译)

【英译】Junzi(a man of virtue) and villain are the same in endowment, nature, intelligence, and capabilities. They both prefer honor and benefits, and they both hate disgrace and dangers, but they differ in their ways of seeking.

(肖莉莉 译)

14 【原文】相形不如论心,论心不如择术。形不胜心,心不胜术。

《荀子·非相》

【今译】观察一个人的外形,不如评论他的思想;评论他的思想,不如考察他的行为。外形不如思想说明问题,思想不如行为说明问题。

（肖莉莉 译）

【英译】Observing one's outer appearance is not as good as evaluating his thought; evaluating one's thought is not as good as inspecting his behavior. To find out about a person, the outer appearance is inferior to thought, and thought is inferior to inspecting one's behavior.

（肖莉莉 译）

15 【原文】形相虽恶而心术善,无害为君子也;形相虽善而心术恶,无害为小人也。

《荀子·非相》

【今译】形象虽然丑陋,但思想端正、心地善良,并不妨碍他成为君子;反之,形象虽好,但心术不正,也不妨碍他成为小人。

（肖莉莉 译）

【英译】If one is ugly in appearance but kind in mind, it will pose no impediment for him to become Junzi(a man of virtue); if one is good in image but ugly in mind, it will pose no impediment for him to become a villain.

（肖莉莉 译）

16 【原文】君子贤而能容罢,知而能容愚,博而能容浅,粹而能容杂,夫是之谓兼术。

《荀子·非相》

【今译】君子贤明而能容纳那些无能的人,有智慧而能容纳那些愚昧的人,学识广博而能容纳那些学识浅薄的人,品行纯洁而能容纳品行驳杂的人,这就是所谓的兼容并蓄。

（肖莉莉 译）

【英译】Junzi(a man of virtue) is competent and worthy but can tolerate the incompetent and the sluggish. He is wise but can tolerate the foolish. He is well-informed but can tolerate the ill-informed. He is pure in morality but can tolerate the impure in morality. This is called ways of inclusiveness.

（肖莉莉 译）

17 【原文】大巧在所不为,大智在所不虑。

《荀子·天论》

【今译】最大的技巧在于没有作为,最大的智慧在于没有考虑。

（肖莉莉 译）

【英译】The greatest skill lies in not doing certain things, and the greatest wisdom lies in not considering certain things.

（肖莉莉 译）

18 【原文】在天者莫明于日月,在地者莫明与水火,在物者莫明于珠玉,在人者莫明于礼义。

《荀子·天论》

【今译】天上没有什么比日月更明亮的了,地上没有什么比水火更明亮的了,万物中没有什么比珠玉更明亮的了,人类社会中没有什么比懂得礼义的君子更明亮的了。

（肖莉莉 译）

【英译】There is no more dazzling than the sun and moon in the heaven; there is no more dazzling than water and fire on the earth; there is no more dazzling than pearls and jade in the universe; there is no more dazzling than Junzi(a man of virtue) who knows the rituals in the human society.

（肖莉莉 译）

19 【原文】君子敬始而慎终。终始如一,是君子之道,礼仪之文也。

《荀子·礼论》

【今译】君子严肃地对待人生的开始,谨慎地对待人生的终结。对生死都一样,这就是君子的处世准则,礼仪的仪式。

（肖莉莉 译）

【英译】Junzi(a man of virtue) takes life seriously and treats death prudently. When beginning and end are treated alike, this is the principle of the Junzi(a man of virtue), and the ritual of the etiquette.

（肖莉莉 译）

20 【原文】夫乐者,乐也,人之情所必不免也,故人不能无乐。乐则必发于声音,形于动静,而人之道,声音、动静、性术之变尽是矣。

《荀子·乐论》

【今译】音乐,是令人快乐的人类情感不可缺少的东西,所以人不能没有音乐。音乐必然在声音上流露出来,表现在人的一举一动中。而人的声音、动静、性格行为的变化,都充分体现在这里了。

（肖莉莉 译）

【英译】Music is a kind of entertainment and an unavoidable human disposition. Hence one cannot live without music. Music will be definitely expressed in sound and displayed in movement. All the changes of sound, movement, character and behavior can find their reflection in music.

（肖莉莉 译）

21 【原文】君子耳不听淫声,目不视邪色,口不出恶言,此三者,君子慎之。

《荀子·乐论》

【今译】君子耳朵不听淫靡的声音,眼睛不看不正的颜色,嘴里不说粗鄙恶毒的话语。这三种行为,君子要慎重对待。

（肖莉莉 译）

【英译】Hence Junzi(a man of virtue) turns a deaf ear to obscene sound, a blind eye to vicious color, and never breaks abusive. Junzi(a man of virtue) is prudent in the above three.

（肖莉莉 译）

22 【原文】夫人虽有性质美而心辩知,必将求贤师而事之,择良友而友之。

《荀子·性恶》

【今译】一个人即使具有良好的素质和辨别能力,也一定要求得贤良的老师向他们学习,选择好的朋友交往。

(肖莉莉 译)

【英译】Even if one has good quality and discernment ability, he also should seek virtuous teacher to serve, and choose worthy friends to befriend.

(肖莉莉 译)

23 【原文】不知其子视其友,不知其君视其左右。

《荀子·性恶》

【今译】不了解他的儿子,观察一下他儿子的朋友就清楚了;不了解他的君主,观察一下君主左右的近臣就清楚了。

(肖莉莉 译)

【英译】If you do not know one's son, observe the son's friends. If you do not know the monarch, observe his companions.

(肖莉莉 译)

24 【原文】善学者尽其理,善行者究其难。

《荀子·大略》

【今译】善于学习的人总会穷究事物的道理,善于行动的人总会探究清楚事物的疑难之处。

(肖莉莉 译)

【英译】Those who are good at learning explore the truth exhaustively. Those who are good at taking actions probe into the difficulty persistently.

(肖莉莉 译)

25 【原文】岁不寒,无以知松柏;事不难,无以知君子。

《荀子·大略》

【今译】不经历寒冬,无法知道松柏的品性;不经过艰难的考验,无法知道君子的品质。

(肖莉莉 译)

【英译】The character of the pine and cypress demonstrates in coldness; likewise, the talent of Junzi(a man of virtue) manifests in hard times.

(肖莉莉 译)

26 【原文】人之于文学也,犹玉之于琢磨也。

《荀子·大略》

【今译】一个人做学问,就像是要琢磨玉石一样精益求精。

(肖莉莉 译)

【英译】One learns literature, just as the jade is carved and polished.

(肖莉莉 译)

27 【原文】学问不厌,好士不倦,是天府也。

《荀子·大略》

【今译】勤学好问而不会满足;喜好贤士而不会厌倦,这就是天然的知识宝库。

(肖莉莉 译)

【英译】To learn diligently and inquiry insatiably, and to associate with distinguished men with fondness tirelessly. This is a heavenly repository.

（肖莉莉 译）

28 【原文】国将兴，必贵师而重傅；……国将衰，必贱师而轻傅。

《荀子·大略》

【今译】国家如果将要振兴，必然倚重教师；……国家如果趋于衰败，必然轻贱教师。

（肖莉莉 译）

【英译】When a country is about to flourish, teachers will surely be honored. ... When a country is about to decline, teachers will surely be belittled.

（肖莉莉 译）

29 【原文】君人者不可以不慎取臣，匹夫不可以不慎取友。

《荀子·大略》

【今译】君主不能不慎重地选择臣子，普通人不能不慎重地选择朋友。

（肖莉莉 译）

【英译】A monarch must choose his ministers prudently, and a commoner must choose his friends carefully.

（肖莉莉 译）

30 【原文】无用吾之所短遇人之所长。

《荀子·大略》

【今译】不要用自己的短处去和别人的长处较量。

（肖莉莉 译）

【英译】One shouldn't tackle with others' merits with one's own demerits.

（肖莉莉 译）

31 【原文】芷兰生于深林，非以无人而不芳。

《荀子·宥坐》

【今译】芷兰生长于深林里，不会因为没有人看见它就没有芳香。

（肖莉莉 译）

【英译】The orchids grow deep in forest will not stop being fragrant just because there are no people around to smell it.

（肖莉莉 译）

32 【原文】君子有三思，而不可不思也。少而不学，长无能也；老而不教，死无思也；有而不施，穷无与也。

《荀子·法行》

【今译】君子有三个方面需要思考，而不能不思考。年少的时候不努力学习，长大了就没有才能；年老的时候不教育后人，死后就没有人想念他；富有的时候不施舍，贫穷的时候就没有人接济他。

（肖莉莉 译）

【英译】Junzi (a man of virtue) must not fail to take three aspects into consideration. If one does not study when young, then when grown he will have no abilities. If one does not instruct others when old, then after death he will not be missed by others. If one does not exercise generosity when he is rich, then when he is impoverished nobody will give to him.

（肖莉莉 译）

（十三）《礼记》
The Book of Rites

1 【原文】虽有嘉肴，弗食，不知其旨也；虽有至道，弗学，不知其善也。是故学然后知不足，教然后知困。知不足，然后能自反也；知困，然后能自强也。故曰：教学相长也。

《礼记·学记》

【今译】尽管有美味可口的菜肴，但不去品尝，就不知道它的味道；尽管有至高的道，但不去学习，就不知道它的好处。所以，学习之后才知道自己的不足，教学然后才知道自己有困惑不解的地方。知道了自己的不足，然后就能自我反省；知道了自己困惑不解的地方，然后才能勉励自己。所以说教和学是相互促进的。

（肖莉莉 译）

【英译】However delicious the food be, if one does not eat, he will never know its taste; However impeccable the Dao(Confucian doctrines) be, if one does not learn it, he will never know its benefits. Therefore the more one learns, the more he sees his deficiency; the more one teachs, the more he finds his bewilderment. Only by knowing his deficiency can he reflect profoundly. Only by knowing his bewilderment can he strengthen himeself. Hence it is said, to teach is to learn.

（肖莉莉 译）

2 【原文】不兴其艺，不能乐学。

《礼记·学记》

【今译】如果对所倡导的各种技艺不是由衷的喜欢，就不会乐于所学。

（肖莉莉 译）

【英译】One will not enjoy learning if he does not relish the various espoused arts.

（肖莉莉 译）

3 【原文】凡学之道，严师为难。师严然后道尊。道尊然后民知敬学。

《礼记·学记》

【今译】凡从师学习最难做到的是尊敬教师。教师受到尊敬，那么教师所传授的道才会受到尊崇；道受到尊崇，然后民众才懂得敬重学业。

（肖莉莉 译）

【英译】With regard to learning, the most difficult thing lies in honoring teachers. Only teachers are honored can Dao(Confucian doctrines) be held in high esteem. Only Dao (Confucian doctrines) is held in high esteem can people respect learning.

（肖莉莉 译）

4 【原文】今之教者,呻其占毕,多其讯言,及于数进,而不顾其安,使人不由其诚,教人不尽其材,其施之也悖,其求之也佛。夫然,故隐其学而疾其师,苦其难而不知其益也。虽终其业,其去之必速,教之不刑,其此之由乎!

《礼记·学记》

【今译】现在一般的教师,只吟诵竹简上的文字照本宣科,说的话大多是责备、数落。并且急于赶进度,而不顾及学生对学得的知识是否掌握和巩固,使得学生学习没有什么主动性,教导学生时不能充分发挥他们的聪明才智,施事这种教育方法既违背了教学原则,学生的学习也不得法。这样一来,学生就会厌恶学习而且憎恨老师,感觉学习艰苦并且体会不到学习的好处。学生即使修完了学业,也会很快忘掉。教育教学没有成效,大概原因就在于此吧。

(张龑真 译)

【英译】Nowadays, ordinary teachers only echo what the books say and most of what they say is to blame and scold. They are eager to catch up, regardless of whether students have mastered or consolidated the knowledge they have learned. Therefore, students have no initiative in learning. The implementation of this teaching method which violates the teaching principle can not give full play to the students' intelligence nor equip the students with appropriate learning method. In this way, students will feel hard to learn and do not realize the benefits of learning, which makes them tired of study and hate teachers. Even if they have completed the course, they will soon forget what they have learned. This may be the reason why education and teaching are not effective.

(张龑真 译)

(十四)《大学》
The Great Learning

1 【原文】大学之道,在明明德,在亲民,在止于至善。

《大学》

【今译】大学的宗旨在于彰显自身的美德,在于使人革旧图新,在于使人达到善的最高境界。

(肖莉莉 译)

【英译】What the great learning aims, is to carry forward virtue; to renovate the people; and to attain the summit of excellence.

(肖莉莉 译)

2 【原文】古之欲明明德于天下者,先治其国;欲治其国者,先齐其家;欲齐其家者,先修其身;欲修其身者,先正其心;欲正其心者,先诚其意;欲诚其意者,先致其知。致知在格物。

《大学》

【今译】古代那些想要把美德彰显于天下的人,首先要治理好自己的国家;要想治理好自己的国家,就先要整治好自己的家庭;要想整治好自己的家庭,就先要提高自身的品德修养;要想提高自身的品德修养,就先要端正自己的心志;要想端正自己的心志,就先要使自己的意念真诚;要想使自己的意念真诚,就必须先获得知识;而获得知识的途径在于穷究事物的根本道理。

(肖莉莉 译)

【英译】The ancients who desired to shine virtue throughout the land, would first govern well their own states. Wishing to govern well their states, they would first regulate their families; wishing to regulate their families, they would first cultivate themselves; wishing to cultivate themselves, they would first rectify their hearts; wishing to rectify their hearts, they would first seek to be sincere in their thoughts; wishing to be sincere in their thoughts, they would first obtain knowledge to the utmost. Knowledge can be obtained only when one explores the way of things.

(肖莉莉 译)

3 【原文】物格而后知至,知至而后意诚,意诚而后心正,心正而后身修,身修而后家齐,家齐而后国治,国治而后天下平。

《大学》

【今译】通过穷究事物的根本道理才能获得知识;获得知识后意念才能真诚;意念真诚后才能思想端正;思想端正后才能修养品性;品性修养后才能整治好家庭;整治好家庭才能治理好国家;治理好国家后才能天下太平。

(肖莉莉 译)

【英译】The extension of knowledge can be achieved only when one explores the way of things. Sincere thoughts can be formed only when knowledge is obtained. The hearts can be rectified only when sincerity is formed in thought. One can cultivate himself only when the heart is rectified. One can manage his family only when he cultivates himself. One can govern well the state only when he can manage his family. The whole world will be tranquil only when the state is rightly governed.

(肖莉莉 译)

4 【原文】自天子以至于庶人,壹是皆以修身为本。其本乱,而末治者否矣。其所厚者薄,而其所薄者厚,未之有也。

《大学》

【今译】从天子到普通老百姓,人人都要以修养品性为根本。根本乱了,要做好枝节的事是不可能的。本该重视的受到轻视,本该轻视的反倒受到重视,这样能把事情做好是从来没有过的。

(肖莉莉 译)

【英译】From the son of heaven down to the the mass of the people, all must consider self-cultivation as the root of everything. When the root is upset, it is not likely that what stems from it will be well managed. It never has been a good case if one treats lightly what is of most importance and greatly cares for what is of secondary importance.

（肖莉莉 译）

5 【原文】《康诰》曰："克明德。"《太甲》曰："顾諟天之明命。"《帝典》曰："克明峻德。"皆自明也。

《大学》

【今译】《康诰》上说："要彰显光明（美好）的品德。"《太甲》上说："顾念上天赋予的光明德性。"《尧典》上说："能够弘扬崇高的品德。"说的都是要弘扬自己的美德。

（肖莉莉 译）

【英译】*The Mandate to Kang* says, "He is able to illustrate the virtue." *Taijia* says："He always keeps his eyes on the virtue bestowed by Heaven." *The Decree of Yao* says；"He is able to make illustrious his lofty virtues." These all show how those people intend to carry forward virtues.

（肖莉莉 译）

6 【原文】汤之《盘铭》曰："苟日新，日日新，又日新。"《康诰》曰："作新民。"《诗》曰："周虽旧邦，其命维新。"是故君子无所不用其极。

《大学》

【今译】商汤刻在浴盆上的警辞说："如果能在一天内做到洁净，就应该坚持天天清洗，做到每日都焕然一新。"《康诰》上说："要激励人民悔过自新。"《诗》上说："周朝虽是古老的邦国，却秉承天命而除旧布新。"可见君子处处用尽心力做到至善的境地。

（肖莉莉 译）

【英译】*The Bathtub Inscription* of Shang Tang says："If one can renovate for one day, do so from day to day, and then renovate constantly." *The Mandate to Kang* says, "To stir up the people to renovate." *The Book of Poetry* says："Although Zhou was an ancient state, it took kismet and obtained a new decree." Hence it is evident that the virtuous people resort to every possible means for perfection.

（肖莉莉 译）

7 【原文】有斐君子，如切如磋，如琢如磨。

《大学》

【今译】有位文采风流的君子，他（治学）如切锉骨器那样严谨，（修身）如琢磨美玉那样精细。

（肖莉莉 译）

【英译】Here is our elegant Junzi(a man of virtue), like ivory being cut and filed, like jade being carved and polished.

（肖莉莉 译）

8 【原文】"如切如磋"者，道学也；"如琢如磨"者，自修也；"瑟兮僩兮"者，恂栗也；"赫兮喧兮"者，威仪也；"有斐君子，终不可喧兮"者，道盛德至善，民之不能忘也。

《大学》

【今译】"如切如磋"，比喻精心求学的方法；"如琢如磨"，比喻修养德性的精神；"瑟兮僩兮"，是指他内心谨慎；"赫兮喧兮"，是指他仪表威严；"有斐君子，终不可喧兮"，是指由于他品德非常高尚，达到了最完美的境界，所以令人难以忘怀。

（肖莉莉 译）

【英译】The so-called "like ivory being cut and filed" indicates the way of learning; "like jade being carved and polished" demonstrates the way one cultivates his mind; "being majestic and dignified" describes the feeling of cautious reverence at heart; "being grandeur and distinguished" describes the impressive manner; "the brilliant Junzi(a man of virtue) never can be forgotten" manifests that the people can never forget his abundant virtues.

（肖莉莉 译）

9 【原文】故君子必慎其独也。

《大学》

【今译】所以,君子在独处的时候,也一定要谨慎。

（肖莉莉 译）

【英译】Hence Junzi(a man of virtue) must be watchful over himself when he is alone.

（肖莉莉 译）

10 【原文】富润屋,德润身,心广体胖,故君子必诚其意。

《大学》

【今译】财富可以润饰房屋,品德却可以修养身心,心胸宽广才能身体舒泰。所以,君子必须要使自己的意念真诚。

（肖莉莉 译）

【英译】Riches adorn a house, while virtue adorns a person which will expand the mind and make the body at ease. Hence Junzi(a man of virtue) will make his thoughts sincere.

（肖莉莉 译）

11 【原文】心不在焉,视而不见,听而不闻,食而不知其味。此谓修身在正其心。

《大学》

【今译】思想不集中,看到了却像没有看到一样;听到了却像没有听到一样;吃东西却不知道食物是什么滋味。所以说,要修养自身的品行,首先要端正自己的心志。

（肖莉莉 译）

【英译】When the mind is absent, he may look but does not see; he may hear but does not understand; he may eat but does not know the taste. This is what is meant by saying that moral cultivation depends on the rectifying of the mind.

（肖莉莉 译）

12 【原文】所谓齐其家在修其身者,人之其所亲爱而辟焉,之其所贱恶而辟焉,之其所畏敬而辟焉,之其所哀矜而辟焉,之其所敖惰而辟焉。

《大学》

【今译】之所以说整治好家庭要先修养自身,是说人们对于自己亲近的人往往会有所偏爱;对于自己厌恶的人往往有所鄙视;对于自己敬重的人往往过分敬畏;对于自己同情的人往往过分怜悯;对于自己轻视的人往往过分怠慢。

（肖莉莉 译）

【英译】What is meant by "The regulation of family depends upon the cultivation of virtue" goes like this: One tends to show affection for those they love, to show hatred against those they dislike, to show reverence for those they stand in awe, to show compassion for those they feel sorrow, to show arrogance to those they despise.

（肖莉莉 译）

13 【原文】故好而知其恶，恶而知其美者，天下鲜矣。

《大学》

【今译】所以很少有人能喜好一个人又看到那人的短处，厌恶一个人又知道那人的长处。

（肖莉莉 译）

【英译】Thus there are few in the world who find bad qualities in those they like, and at the same time know the good qualities in those they dislike.

（肖莉莉 译）

14 【原文】故谚有之曰："人莫知其子之恶，莫知其苗之硕。"此谓身不修不可以齐其家。

《大学》

【今译】所以有条谚语说："人们都不知道自己孩子的坏处，人们都不满足自己禾苗的茂盛。"这就是不修养自身就不能整治好家庭的道理。

（肖莉莉 译）

【英译】As the proverb says, "None will know wickedness of his own children, and none will satisty the growth of his corn." This is what is meant by saying that one cannot regulate his family if he can not first cultivate himself.

（肖莉莉 译）

15 【原文】所谓治国必先齐其家者，其家不可教而能教人者，无之。

《大学》

【今译】所谓治理国家必须先整治好自己的家庭(族)，是说不能管教好家人而能管教好别人的人，是不存在的。

（肖莉莉 译）

【英译】When we say "One who intends to govern his country rightly should first regulate his family well," we mean that a man cannot possibly instruct others if he fails to educate his own family.

（肖莉莉 译）

16 【原文】故君子不出家而成教于国。孝者，所以事君也；悌者，所以事长也；慈者，所以使众也。

《大学》

【今译】所以，有修养的人不出家门也能收到治理国家的成效。对父母的孝顺可以用来侍奉君主；对兄长的尊敬可以用来侍奉长辈；对子女的慈爱可以用来对待百姓。

（肖莉莉 译）

【英译】Therefore, Junzi (a man of virtue) completes the instruction for state governance without going beyond his own family. Filial piety to parents may serve the sovereign; fraternal love may serve elders and superiors; affection for children may serve the people.

（肖莉莉 译）

17 【原文】《康诰》曰："如保赤子。"心诚求之，虽不中不远矣。

《大学》

【今译】《康诰》说："保护百姓就如同爱护婴儿一样。"心中真诚地去追求，即使达不到目标，也会相差不远。

（肖莉莉 译）

【英译】*The Mandate to Kang* says: "Nourish the people the way a mother cares for her tender offspring." One with a sincere heart will be close to his goal even though he can not reach it.

（肖莉莉 译）

18 【原文】一家仁，一国兴仁；一家让，一国兴让；一人贪戾，一国作乱：其机如此。

《大学》

【今译】一家讲求仁爱，一国就会兴起仁爱的风气；一家讲求礼让，一国就会兴起礼让的风气；君主一人贪婪暴戾，一国的国民就会犯上作乱。其影响必然如此。

（肖莉莉 译）

【英译】If each family is benevolent, then the whole nation will flourish in benevolence. If each family is polite, then the whole nation will flourish in politeness. If a ruler is avaricious, then the whole state will be led to turmoil. The influence will be a certainty.

（肖莉莉 译）

19 【原文】此谓一言偾事，一人定国。

《大学》

【今译】这就叫作：一句话可以败坏大事，一个人可以安定国家。

（肖莉莉 译）

【英译】This verifies the adage, "a single word may ruin an affair, and a single person may settle a state."

（肖莉莉 译）

20 【原文】尧、舜帅天下以仁，而民从之。桀、纣帅天下以暴，而民从之。

《大学》

【今译】尧舜用仁爱统治天下，老百姓就跟着一起仁爱；桀纣用暴虐统治天下，老百姓就跟着一起暴虐。

（肖莉莉 译）

【英译】Yao and Shun ruled the state with benevolence, and the people imitated them. Jie and Zhou ruled the state by violence, and the people followed them.

（肖莉莉 译）

21 【原文】其所令反其所好，而民不从。

《大学》

【今译】统治者的命令跟他们自己的喜好相反,百姓就不会听从。

（肖莉莉 译）

【英译】When the rulers issue the orders which are contrary to their preferences, the people will not obey.

（肖莉莉 译）

22 【原文】是故君子有诸己而后求诸人,无诸己而后非诸人。

《大学》

【今译】所以,君子自己要具备美好的德行,然后才能要求别人具备这种美好的德行;自己要没有恶劣的德行,然后才要求别人去除这样的德行。

（肖莉莉 译）

【英译】Hence Junzi(a man of virtue) must himself possess good qualities, and then he may call for it in others. He must himself be free from wickedness, and then he may require them in others.

（肖莉莉 译）

23 【原文】故治国在齐其家。

《大学》

【今译】所以,治理国家必须要先管理好自己的家庭。

（肖莉莉 译）

【英译】Hence the good governance of a state depends on the proper regulation of the family.

（肖莉莉 译）

24 【原文】宜其家人,而后可以教国人。

《大学》

【今译】整治好自己的家人,才能够教化一国的人。

（肖莉莉 译）

【英译】If a family can be properly regulated, a state can then be instructed.

（肖莉莉 译）

25 【原文】此谓治国在齐其家。

《大学》

【今译】这就是要治理国家必须首先要整治好自己的家庭的道理。

（肖莉莉 译）

【英译】This is what is meant by saying, "The governance of the state depends on the proper regulation of the family."

（肖莉莉 译）

26 【原文】《诗》云:"宜兄宜弟。"宜兄宜弟,而后可以教国人。

《大学》

【今译】《诗经》说:"兄弟和睦。"兄弟和睦了,然后才能教化一国的人都和睦。

（肖莉莉 译）

【英译】*The Book of Poetry* says: "Let there be harmony among the brothers."

Make sure that there is harmony among the brothers, and you will be eligible to instruct the whole nation to be harmonious.

（肖莉莉 译）

27 【原文】《诗》云："其仪不忒，正是四国。"其为父子兄弟足法，而后民法之也。此谓治国在齐其家。

《大学》

【今译】《诗经》说："礼仪没有差错，才能成为四方各国的表率。"只有当一个人无论是作为父亲、儿子，还是兄长、弟弟时都值得效法时，老百姓才会去效法他。这就是要治理国家必须先整治好家庭的道理。

（肖莉莉 译）

【英译】*The Book of Poetry* says: "One who demonstrates faultless deportment will rectify the people of the state." One who conducts as an example to all as a father, a son, an elder and younger brother will be worthy of imitation, and the people will follow his example. This is what is meant by saying, "The government of the state depends on the proper regulation of the family."

（肖莉莉 译）

28 【原文】所谓平天下在治其国者，上老老而民兴孝，上长长而民兴悌，上恤孤而民不倍，是以君子有絜矩之道也。

《大学》

【今译】所谓平定天下在于治理好自己的国家，是说在上位的人孝敬老人，老百姓就会孝敬自己的父母，在上位的人敬重长辈，老百姓就会敬重自己的兄长；在上位的人怜恤孤儿，老百姓就不会背道而行。所以，君子总是在道德上起到示范作用。

（肖莉莉 译）

【英译】When we say "The pacifying of the world depends on the government of the state", we mean that when the sovereign respects the aged, the people will abide by filial piety; when the sovereign respects the elders, the people will demonstrate fraternal love; when the sovereign sympathizes with the helpless, the people will not run contrary to it. Hence Junzi(a man of virtue) serves as a model by regulating his conduct.

（肖莉莉 译）

29 【原文】所恶于上，毋以使下，所恶于下，毋以事上；所恶于前，毋以先后；所恶于后，毋以从前；所恶于右，毋以交于左；所恶于左，毋以交于右；此之谓絜矩之道。

《大学》

【今译】如果厌恶上司对你所做的一切，就不要这样去对待你的下属；如果厌恶下属对你所做的一切，就不要这样去对待你的上司；如果厌恶你前面的人对你所做的一切，就不要这样去对待你后面的人；如果厌恶你后面的人对你所做的一切，就不要这样去对待你前面的人；如果厌恶你右边的人对你所做的一切，就不要这样去对待你左边的人；如果厌恶你左边的人对你所做的一切，就不要这样去对待你右边的人。这就是所说的君子在道德上的示范作用。

（肖莉莉 译）

【英译】If you hate what your superiors do to you, never display the same to your inferiors; if you hate what your inferiors do to you, never display the same to your superiors; if you hate what the one before you do to you, never display the same to those behind you; if you hate what those on your right do to you, never display the same to those on your left; if you hate what those on your left do to you, never display the same to those on your right. That is what is called "Junzi(a man of virtue) serves as a model by regulating his conduct. "

(肖莉莉 译)

30 【原文】《诗》云:"乐只君子,民之父母。"

《大学》

【今译】《诗经》上说:"有这样的国君多好啊,他是天下百姓的父母。"

(肖莉莉 译)

【英译】The Book of Poetry says: "How pleasant is it when a sovereign is the parent of the people! "

(肖莉莉 译)

31 【原文】民之所好好之,民之所恶恶之,此之谓民之父母。

《大学》

【今译】老百姓喜爱的,他也喜爱;老百姓厌恶的,他也厌恶,这才叫作老百姓的父母。

(肖莉莉 译)

【英译】One who loves what the people love, and hates what the people hate, is the parent of the people.

(肖莉莉 译)

32 【原文】《诗》云:"节彼南山,维石岩岩。"

《大学》

【今译】《诗经》上说:"巍峨高大的南山啊,险峻的岩石层层耸立。"

(肖莉莉 译)

【英译】The Book of Poetry says: "How lofty is that south mountain with rugged rocks!"

(肖莉莉 译)

33 【原文】《诗》云:"赫赫师尹,民具尔瞻。"

《大学》

【今译】《诗经》上说:"权势显赫的尹太师啊,百姓都用恐惧愤怒的目光注视着你。"

(肖莉莉 译)

【英译】The Book of Poetry says: "Such is the minacious minister Yin! The people all look up to you with terror and anger!"

(肖莉莉 译)

34 【原文】有国者不可以不慎,辟则为天下僇矣。

《大学》

【今译】掌握国家大权的人不可不谨慎。一旦出现偏差,就会被天下人杀戮。

(肖莉莉 译)

【英译】The ruler of a state may not neglect to be cautious. If he deviates from the right path, he will be killed by the people.

(肖莉莉 译)

35 【原文】《诗》云:"殷之未丧师,克配上帝。仪监于殷,峻命不易。"

《大学》

【今译】《诗经》上说:"殷朝尚未丧失民心的时候,还能够与上天的要求符合。以殷商的兴亡为鉴戒吧,守住天命并非易事。"

(肖莉莉 译)

【英译】*The Book of Poetry* says: "Before the Yin Dynasty lost the hearts of the people, it still conformed to God of Heaven. Look at Yin as a mirror! Observing the decree of Heaven would be a tough task."

(肖莉莉 译)

36 【原文】道得众则得国,失众则失国。

《大学》

【今译】得民心者得天下,失民心者失天下。

(肖莉莉 译)

【英译】One who gains the support of the people gains the state, and one who loses the support of the people loses the state.

(肖莉莉 译)

37 【原文】是故君子先慎乎德。

《大学》

【今译】所以,君子首先要注重道德修养。

(肖莉莉 译)

【英译】Hence Junzi(a man of virtue) will first approach virtue seriously.

(肖莉莉 译)

38 【原文】有德此有人,有人此有土,有土此有财,有财此有用。

《大学》

【今译】有了道德才会拥有人民,有了人民才能拥有土地,有了土地才会拥有财富,有了财富才能国用充足。

(肖莉莉 译)

【英译】One who possesses virtue obtains the people. One who possesses the people obtains the territory. One who possesses the territory obtains the wealth. One who possesses the wealth obtains sufficient supplies.

(肖莉莉 译)

39 【原文】德者本也,财者末也。外本内末,争民施夺。

《大学》

【今译】道德是根本,财富是枝末,轻根本而重枝末,那就会和老百姓争夺利益。

(肖莉莉 译)

【英译】Virtue is the root and wealth is the branches. If you reverse them by putting the branches before the root, you will contend for wealth with the people.

(肖莉莉 译)

40 【原文】是故财聚则民散,财散则民聚。

《大学》

【今译】所以,君王聚敛财富,民心就会失散;君王散财于民,民心就会聚拢。

(肖莉莉 译)

【英译】Hence the accumulation of wealth may scatter the people; and the diffusing of wealth may assemble the people.

(肖莉莉 译)

41 【原文】是故言悖而出者,亦悖而入;货悖而入者,亦悖而出。

《大学》

【今译】所以你说话不讲道理,人家也会用不讲道理的话来回敬你;财货以一种不合理的方式得到,最终也会以一种不合理的方式失去。

(肖莉莉 译)

【英译】Hence unreasonable remarks will receive unreasonable response, and obtaining wealth in an irrational way will finally end in losing it in the same irrational way.

(肖莉莉 译)

42 【原文】《康诰》曰:"惟命不于常。"

《大学》

【今译】《康诰》上说:"天命不会总是护佑我们。"

(肖莉莉 译)

【英译】*The Mandate to Kang* says, "Kismet may not always rest on us."

(肖莉莉 译)

43 【原文】道善则得之,不善则失之矣。

《大学》

【今译】行善便会得到天命,不行善便会失去天命。

(肖莉莉 译)

【英译】Approaching virtue obtains kismet, while turning away from virtue loses kismet.

(肖莉莉 译)

44 【原文】《楚书》曰:"楚国无以为宝,惟善以为宝。"

《大学》

【今译】《楚书》上说:"楚国没有什么可以当作宝贝,只是把'善'当作宝贝。"

(肖莉莉 译)

【英译】The *Book of Chu* says:"The State of Chu values nothing precious but virtue."

(肖莉莉 译)

45【原文】舅犯曰:"亡人无以为宝,仁亲以为宝。"

《大学》

【今译】(晋公子重耳的)舅舅子犯说:"流亡在外的人没有什么可以当作宝贝,只有把仁爱之心当作宝贝。"

(肖莉莉 译)

【英译】Uncle Zifan said, "The exiles value nothing precious except affection for parents."

(肖莉莉 译)

46【原文】《秦誓》曰:"若有一介臣,断断兮无他技,其心休休焉,其如有容焉。"

《大学》

【今译】《秦誓》上说:"假如有这样一位大臣,老实诚挚,虽然没有什么特别的本领,但他心胸宽广,有容人之量。"

(肖莉莉 译)

【英译】*The Pledge of Qin* says: "Let me have such a minister, honest and sincere, devoid of other abilities, but broad-minded and generous."

(肖莉莉 译)

47【原文】人之有技,若己有之;人之彦圣,其心好之,不啻若自其口出。

《大学》

【今译】别人有本领,就好像他自己有本领一样;别人德才兼备,他从内心赞赏而不只是口头上称赞。

(肖莉莉 译)

【英译】When one finds a man of immense talents, he will deem his talents as if they are his own. When one comes upon a man of virtue and wisdom, he will not merely praise with his lips, but really admire him from the bottom of his heart.

(肖莉莉 译)

48【原文】实能容之,以能保我子孙黎民,尚亦有利哉!

《大学》

【今译】用这样的人,就能保护我的子孙和百姓,是可以为他们造福的啊!

(肖莉莉 译)

【英译】Such a man can protect my offspring and my people, and will be of great benefits to them.

(肖莉莉 译)

49【原文】人之有技,媢嫉以恶之;人之彦圣,而违之俾不通:实不能容,以不能保我子孙黎民,亦曰殆哉!

《大学》

【今译】假设别人有本领,他就厌恶和妒忌;别人德才兼备,他就加以阻挠使之接触不到国君,这种人我不能容纳,因为他不能保护我的子孙和百姓,而且对国家危险啊。

(肖莉莉 译)

【英译】Let's suppose here is another minister who hates and is jealous of men of talents, and opposes those accomplished and virtuous by hindering their contacts with the sovereign. I really cannot accept such a man because he is incapable of protecting my offspring and my people, and will be dangerous to the state.

（肖莉莉 译）

50 【原文】唯仁人放流之，迸诸四夷，不与同中国。此谓唯仁人为能爱人，能恶人。

《大学》

【今译】只有仁德的人才会把这种人流放，把他们驱逐到边远荒蛮的地方，不让他们同中原人民住在一起。这就是说，只有仁德的人能够爱护好人，憎恶坏人。

（肖莉莉 译）

【英译】It is only the virtuous man who will banish such a minister, expelling him to a far-flung and isolated place, banning him from dwelling in the central land. This is in line with the saying, "Only a man of benevolence can either cherish the virtuous or abhor the evil."

（肖莉莉 译）

51 【原文】见贤而不能举，举而不能先，命也；见不善而不能退，退而不能远，过也。

《大学》

【今译】发现贤才而不能荐举，荐举了而不能重用，这是怠慢；发现恶人而不能把他罢退，罢退了而不能把他放逐得远远的，这是过错。

（肖莉莉 译）

【英译】This can be impropriety if one acts as a talent scout but fails to promote the talent to office, or promotes the talent to office but fails to give priority to his post. This can be a fault if one finds a man devoid of virtue but fails to send him away, or sends him away but fails to send him to a great distance.

（肖莉莉 译）

52 【原文】好人之所恶，恶人之所好，是谓拂人之性，灾必逮夫身。

《大学》

【今译】喜爱人们所憎恶的，憎恶人们所喜爱的，这就是违背人的本性，灾难必然要降临在自己身上。

（肖莉莉 译）

【英译】If one loves what others hate, and hates what others love, he is outraging the human nature. Disaster will definitely fall on such a man.

（肖莉莉 译）

53 【原文】是故君子有大道，必忠信以得之，骄泰以失之。

《大学》

【今译】因此做国君的要遵循一个大的原则：忠诚信义就会获得一切；骄傲自大，奢侈放纵就会失去一切。

（肖莉莉 译）

【英译】Hence a sovereign adheres to such a general principle: He must hold fast to loyalty and sincerity by which he gains, and will lose due to arrogance and extravagance.

（肖莉莉 译）

54 【原文】生财有大道,生之者众,食之者寡,为之者疾,用之者舒,则财恒足矣。

《大学》

【今译】创造财富也有正确的途径:要使创造财富的人多,消耗财富的人少;生产财富的人变得勤奋,动用财富的人持守节俭。这样财用便时时充足。

(肖莉莉 译)

【英译】There are right ways of creating wealth: let the creators be many, the consumers be few, the producers be diligent and the users be economical. In this way the wealth will always be sufficient.

(肖莉莉 译)

55 【原文】仁者以财发身,不仁者以身发财。

《大学》

【今译】有仁德的人散财于民以提升自身,没有仁德的人贬损自身去聚敛财富。

(肖莉莉 译)

【英译】A virtuous ruler promotes himself by means of his wealth, while a vicious ruler accumulates wealth at the expense of degrading himself.

(肖莉莉 译)

56 【原文】未有上好仁而下不好义者也,未有好义其事不终者也,未有府库财非其财者也。

《大学》

【今译】从没听说过国君喜爱仁德而臣民却不喜爱仁义的;从没听说过喜爱仁义,而不能完成其事业的;从没听说过国库里的财物不是属于国君的。

(肖莉莉 译)

【英译】It has never occured that when the sovereign values benevolence, and the people despise righteousness; it has never occured that when the people love justice, and the affairs fail to be carried out. And never has there been a case where the treasury in a state does not belong to the sovereign.

(肖莉莉 译)

57 【原文】孟献子曰:"畜马乘不察于鸡豚,伐冰之家不畜牛羊,百乘之家不畜聚敛之臣。与其有聚敛之臣,宁有盗臣。"

《大学》

【今译】孟献子说:"拥有车马的士大夫家,不可再去计较饲养鸡豚的小事;祭祀时能用冰的卿大夫之家,不应该饲养牛羊;拥有百辆兵车的诸侯之家,不应该豢养搜刮民财的家臣。与其养几个搜刮民财的家臣,还不如养几个盗窃府库财物的家臣。"

(肖莉莉 译)

【英译】Meng Xianzi once said, "One who keeps horses and carriages ought not to care about fowls and pigs. One who uses ice in their sacrifices ought not to rear cattle and sheep. A family of a hundred chariots ought not to keep retainers to plunder money from the people for them. Keeping such rapacious retainers is even worse than keeping some stealing retainers."

(肖莉莉 译)

58 【原文】此谓国不以利为利,以义为利也。

《大学》

【今译】这就是说,一个国家不应该以财货为利,而应该以正义为利。

(肖莉莉 译)

【英译】This is in line with the saying, "It is by righteousness, not by profits that a state is benefited."

(肖莉莉 译)

59 【原文】长国家而务财用者,必自小人矣。彼为善之,小人之使为国家,灾害并至。虽有善者,亦无如之何矣!此谓国不以利为利,以义为利也。

《大学》

【今译】国君一心想着聚敛财富,这必然是受小人的影响,而那国君还以为这些小人是心存善良的人,让他们去处理国家大事,因此天灾人祸一齐降临。这时即便有贤能的人,也是无能为力了。这说明一个国家不应该以财货为利,而应该以仁义为利。

(肖莉莉 译)

【英译】When a sovereign is wrapped up in the accumulation of wealth, he must be swayed by some vicious fellows. He may see these base person as men of kindness, and put the state in their hands, thus natural calamities and man-made misfortunes will befall together. Then even a virtuous and talented man will be powerless to remedy the evil. This manifests again the saying, "It is by righteousness, not by profits that a state is benefited."

(肖莉莉 译)

(十五)《中庸》
Doctrine of the Mean

1 【原文】是故君子戒慎乎其所不睹,恐惧乎其所不闻。

《中庸》

【今译】所以君子在没有人看到的地方,也要保持谨慎检点;在没有人听到的地方,也要心存戒惧。

(肖莉莉 译)

【英译】Hence Junzi(a man of virtue) still maintains cautious when he is out of sight of others, and awed when he is out of sound of others.

(肖莉莉 译)

2 【原文】莫见乎隐,莫显乎微。故君子慎其独也。

《中庸》

【今译】无论多么隐秘的事物,也难免要现形;无论多么微小的事物,也一定会显露,所以君子独处的时候应该警惕谨慎。

(肖莉莉 译)

【英译】No matter how secret it is, it will inevitably be revealed; no matter how minute it is, it will definitely show its true colors. Hence Junzi(a man of virtue) ought to be watchful over himself when he is alone.

（肖莉莉 译）

3 【原文】中也者,天下之大本也;和也者,天下之达道也。

《中庸》

【今译】"中"是天下万物的根本,"和"是天下共行的普遍原则。

（肖莉莉 译）

【英译】Moderation is the root of all things, and harmony is the universal principle of the world.

（肖莉莉 译）

4 【原文】致中和,天地位焉,万物育焉。

《中庸》

【今译】如果能达到"中和"的境界,那么天地就能各得其所,万物就能生长了。

（肖莉莉 译）

【英译】If a combination of moderation and harmony exists in perfection, heaven and earth will be in order and all things will be produced and flourish.

（肖莉莉 译）

5 【原文】子曰:"中庸其至矣乎! 民鲜能久矣!"

《中庸》

【今译】孔子说:"中庸是最高的道德了,可是人们却很少能达到这种状态了。"

（肖莉莉 译）

【英译】Confucius remarks, "Perfect is the doctrine of the mean! But rare has it long been among the people!"

（肖莉莉 译）

6 【原文】子曰:"道之不行也,我知之矣,知者过之,愚者不及也。"

《中庸》

【今译】孔子说:"中庸之道不能实行于世的原因,我知道了:聪明的人过于聪明,超过限度;愚蠢的人不够聪明,不能理解它。"

（肖莉莉 译）

【英译】Confucius remarks, "I know the reason why the doctrine of the mean cannot be carried out. This is because the knowing go beyond it, and the foolish cannot reach it."

（肖莉莉 译）

7 【原文】子曰:"道之不明也,我知之矣:贤者过之,不肖者不及也。"

《中庸》

【今译】孔子说:"中庸之道不能实行于世的原因,我知道了:贤能的人做得过了头,没有贤德的人又做不到。"

（肖莉莉 译）

【英译】Confucius remarks, "I know the reason why the doctrine of the mean cannot be pervasive. This is because the virtuous go beyond it, and the worthless cannot reach it."

（肖莉莉 译）

8 【原文】子曰："人莫不饮食也，鲜能知味也。"

《中庸》

【今译】孔子说："就像人们每天都要吃喝，但很少有人能够知道真正的滋味。"

（肖莉莉 译）

【英译】Confucius remarks, "Everyone eats and drinks, but few know the real flavors."

（肖莉莉 译）

9 【原文】执其两端，用其中于民。

《中庸》

【今译】他平衡事物的两个极端，采用不偏不倚的方式来治理百姓。

（肖莉莉 译）

【英译】He balanced the two extremes of things and avoided leaning to either side so as to regulate the people.

（肖莉莉 译）

10 【原文】故君子和而不流，强哉矫！

《中庸》

【今译】所以君子平和而不随波逐流，这才是真正的强大啊！

（肖莉莉 译）

【英译】Hence Junzi(a man of virtue) takes hold of moderation, without following the beaten track. How firm and unbending he is!

（肖莉莉 译）

11 【原文】中立而不倚，强哉矫！

《中庸》

【今译】保持中立而不偏不倚，这才是真正的强大啊！

（肖莉莉 译）

【英译】Junzi(a man of virtue) stands in the middle without inclining to either side. How firm and unbending he is!

（肖莉莉 译）

12 【原文】国有道，不变塞焉，强哉矫！

《中庸》

【今译】国家政治清明时，即使遭受困厄也坚持操守，这才是真正的强大啊！

（肖莉莉 译）

【英译】When integrity and pureness prevail in his state, he adheres to his aspiration even in times of hardship. How firm and unbending he is!

（肖莉莉 译）

13 【原文】国无道,至死不变,强哉矫!

《中庸》

【今译】国家政治黑暗时,至死也不改变自己的操守,这才是真正的强大啊!

(肖莉莉 译)

【英译】When the state deviates from the right path, he will never change even till death. How firm and unbending he is!

(肖莉莉 译)

14 【原文】子曰:"素隐行怪,后世有述焉,吾弗为之矣。"

《中庸》

【今译】孔子说:"探求隐僻的道理,做些荒唐怪异之事,后世也许会有人来记述他们,但我不会这样做。"

(肖莉莉 译)

【英译】Confucius remarks, "To bury head in the hidden mysteries, and practise something weird in order to be recorded in future ages, is what I will not do."

(肖莉莉 译)

15 【原文】君子遵道而行,半途而废,吾弗能已矣。

《中庸》

【今译】君子按照中庸之道来行事,有些人半途而废,但我是永远不会停息的。

(肖莉莉 译)

【英译】Junzi(a man of virtue) follows the doctrine of the mean in his conduct. Some give up halfway, but I will not follow suit.

(肖莉莉 译)

16 【原文】君子依乎中庸,遁世不见知而不悔,唯圣者能之。

《中庸》

【今译】君子遵循中庸之道行事,即使默默无闻不被人知也不后悔,这只有圣人能做得到。

(肖莉莉 译)

【英译】Junzi(a man of virtue) accords with the doctrine of the mean, and feels no regret even though he may be unknown to the world. It is only the sage who can act this way.

(肖莉莉 译)

17 【原文】君子之道费而隐。

《中庸》

【今译】君子所遵循的中庸之道,广大无涯而又精微奥妙。

(肖莉莉 译)

【英译】The doctrine of the mean which Junzi(a man of virtue) adheres to reaches far, and yet is subtle and profound.

(肖莉莉 译)

18 【原文】《诗》云:'鸢飞戾天,鱼跃于渊。'言其上下察也。

《中庸》

【今译】《诗经》上说:"老鹰高飞上青天,鱼儿跳跃入深渊。"这是说中庸之道上达于天,下及于渊。

(肖莉莉 译)

【英译】*The Book of Poetry* says,"Eagles fly up to heaven and fishes leap in the deep. " This illustrates how the doctrine of the mean is revealed above and below.

(肖莉莉 译)

19 【原文】子曰:"道不远人。人之为道而远人,不可以为道。"

《中庸》

【今译】孔子说:"中庸之道并未远离人们。如果有人在践行中庸之道时远离他人,那就不叫中庸之道了。"

(肖莉莉 译)

【英译】Confucius remarks," the doctrine of the mean is not far from mankind. When one practices the doctrine of the mean to isolate himself from others, this cannot be considered as the doctrine of the mean. "

(肖莉莉 译)

20 【原文】《诗》云:'伐柯伐柯,其则不远。'执柯以伐柯,睨而视之,犹以为远。

《中庸》

【今译】《诗经》上说:"伐木做斧柄啊,伐木做斧柄,斧柄的式样就在眼前。"握着斧柄砍伐木材制作斧柄,如果斜眼看着手中的斧柄,还是觉得式样远在别处。

(肖莉莉 译)

【英译】*The Book of Poetry* says:"In hewing an ax-handle, the pattern of the ax-handle is not far from you. " When you take hold of one ax-handle, and use it to hew another, looking aslant at it, it will appear distant.

(肖莉莉 译)

21 【原文】故君子以人治人。改而止。

《中庸》

【今译】因此君子用做人的道理来治理人,帮助他们直到改过自新为止。

(肖莉莉 译)

【英译】Hence Junzi(a man of virtue) regulates the people by the principles of being a man, and helps them to turn a new leaf.

(肖莉莉 译)

22 【原文】忠恕违道不远,施诸己而不愿,亦勿施于人。

《中庸》

【今译】能够做到忠恕,那就离中庸之道不远了。不愿意别人强加给自己的行为,也不要强加给别人。

(肖莉莉 译)

【英译】Loyalty and forgiveness are not far from the doctrine of the mean. Do not do to others what you do not want others to impose on you.

（肖莉莉 译）

23 【原文】言顾行,行顾言,君子胡不慥慥尔!

《中庸》

【今译】言语符合自己的行为,行为符合自己的言语,这样的君子怎么会不忠厚老实呢?

（肖莉莉 译）

【英译】If his words are in line with his actions, and his actions are in line with his words, can't we say a Junzi(a man of virtue) like this be upright and honest?

（肖莉莉 译）

24 【原文】在上位不陵下,在下位不援上,正己而不求于人,则无怨。

《中庸》

【今译】身处高位,不欺凌身在井隅的人;身在井隅,不攀附位居高位的人。端正自己而不去苛求别人,这样就不会有什么怨恨了。

（肖莉莉 译）

【英译】In a high position, he does not behave high-handedly toward his inferiors. In the gutter, he does not play up to his superiors. He rectifies himself and not judge others too harshly. In this way he has no resentment.

（肖莉莉 译）

25 【原文】上不怨天,下不尤人。

《中庸》

【今译】上不抱怨苍天,下不抱怨别人。

（肖莉莉 译）

【英译】He grumbles against neither Heaven nor other people.

（肖莉莉 译）

26 【原文】子曰:"射有似乎君子,失诸正鹄,反求诸其身。"

《中庸》

【今译】孔子说:"君子立身处世就像射箭一样,射不中靶子,应该到自己身上去找原因。"

（肖莉莉 译）

【英译】Confucius remarks, "Junzi(a man of virtue) may be compared to an archer. When an archer misses the target, he turns round and seeks the reason of his failure in himself."

（肖莉莉 译）

27 【原文】君子之道,辟如行远必自迩,辟如登高必自卑。

《中庸》

【今译】(践行)中庸之道可比作长途旅行,就好比走远路一定要从近处开始,就好比登高山一定要从低处起步。

（肖莉莉 译）

【英译】Practicing the doctrine of the mean may be compared to a long journey. When you go to a distance you must start at the nearest point, and when you climb high you must begin from low.

（肖莉莉 译）

28 【原文】《诗》曰:"嘉乐君子,宪宪令德!"

《中庸》

【今译】《诗经》上说:"高尚优雅的君子,美德显赫光明!"

（肖莉莉 译）

【英译】*The Book of Poetry* says:"The lofty, graceful Junzi(a man of virtue) displays conspicuously his brilliant virtue!"

（肖莉莉 译）

29 【原文】或生而知之,或学而知之,或困而知之,及其知之,一也。

《中庸》

【今译】有的人生来就有知识,有的人通过学习获得知识,有的人经历困惑后才获得知识;但最终掌握知识后,他们却都是一样的了。

（肖莉莉 译）

【英译】Some are born with the knowledge; some by study attain the knowledge; and some acquire the knowledge after lots of puzzlement and perplexity. But they tend to be the same once knowledge is finally obtained.

（肖莉莉 译）

30 【原文】子曰:"好学近乎知,力行近乎仁,知耻近乎勇。"

《中庸》

【今译】孔子说:"爱好学习,离智慧就不远了;努力行善,离仁义就不远了;知道羞耻,离勇敢就不远了。"

（肖莉莉 译）

【英译】Confucius remarks,"One who loves study, is near knowledge. One who seeks to do good deeds, is near benevolence. One who possesses sense of shame, is near bravery."

（肖莉莉 译）

31 【原文】知斯三者,则知所以修身;知所以修身,则知所以治人;知所以治人,则知所以治天下国家矣。

《中庸》

【今译】知道这三点就知道如何修身,知道如何修身就知道如何管理人民,知道如何管理人民就知道如何治理天下和国家了。

（肖莉莉 译）

【英译】One who knows these three things, knows how to cultivate personal virtue. One who knows how to cultivate personal virtue, knows how to govern the people. One who knows how to govern the people, knows how to govern the world and the state.

（肖莉莉 译）

32 【原文】凡事豫则立,不豫则废。

《中庸》

【今译】任何事情,事先做好准备就会成功,没有准备就会失败。

(肖莉莉 译)

【英译】For all things, beforehand preparation leads to success, while unreadiness leads to failure.

(肖莉莉 译)

33 【原文】言前定则不跲,事前定则不困,行前定则不疚,道前定则不穷。

《中庸》

【今译】说话提前想好说什么就不会语塞中断,做事提前想好做什么就不会陷入困境,提前决定就不会悔恨,提前定下来走哪条道路就不会陷入窘境。

(肖莉莉 译)

【英译】If one's words are previously fixed, there will be no stumbling. If one's affairs are prepared beforehand, there will be no dilemma. If one's actions are previously determined, there will be no regret. If one's paths are prepared in advance, there will be no dead end.

(肖莉莉 译)

34 【原文】在下位不获乎上,民不可得而治矣。

《中庸》

【今译】下级如果得不到上级的信任,那么就管理不好百姓。

(肖莉莉 译)

【英译】When the inferiors fail to obtain reliance of their superiors, they fail to govern the people.

(肖莉莉 译)

35 【原文】获乎上有道:不信乎朋友,不获乎上矣。

《中庸》

【今译】得到上级的信任是有方法的:如果一个人得不到朋友的信任,那他就得不到上级的信任。

(肖莉莉 译)

【英译】There is a way to obtain reliance of the superiors: if one is not trusted by his friends, he will naturally not be trusted by his superiors.

(肖莉莉 译)

36 【原文】信乎朋友有道:不顺乎亲,不信乎朋友矣。

《中庸》

【今译】得到朋友的信任是有方法的:如果一个人不孝顺父母,那他就得不到朋友的信任。

(肖莉莉 译)

【英译】There is a way to be trusted by friends: if one is not filial to his parents, he will not be trusted by his friends.

(肖莉莉 译)

37 【原文】顺乎亲有道：反诸身不诚，不顺乎亲矣。

《中庸》

【今译】孝顺父母是有方法的：如果一个人自己不真诚就不能孝顺父母。

（肖莉莉 译）

【英译】There is a way to be filial to parents: if one is insincere, he will not be filial to his parents.

（肖莉莉 译）

38 【原文】诚身有道：不明乎善，不诚乎身矣。

《中庸》

【今译】使自己心诚是有方法的：不明白什么是善，就不能使自己心诚。

（肖莉莉 译）

【英译】There is a way to be sincere: if one does not clearly understand what is good, he will not attain sincerity in himself.

（肖莉莉 译）

39 【原文】诚者，天之道也；诚之者，人之道也。

《中庸》

【今译】诚实，是天道的法则；做到诚实，是人道的法则。

（肖莉莉 译）

【英译】Sincerity is the way of heaven. The pursuit of sincerity is the way of human.

（肖莉莉 译）

40 【原文】诚者不勉而中，不思而得，从容中道，圣人也。

《中庸》

【今译】真诚的人，不需勉强就合乎中和之道，不需思考就可得到，举止从容合乎中庸之道，这样的人就是圣人。

（肖莉莉 译）

【英译】One who possesses sincerity conforms to moderation without reluctance, obtains without thought, and demonstrates unhurried behavior which accords with the doctrine of the mean. Such is a sage.

（肖莉莉 译）

41 【原文】诚之者，择善而固执之者也。

《中庸》

【今译】要做到真诚，就是要选择善行，然后坚持不懈地做下去。

（肖莉莉 译）

【英译】One who aims at sincerity is the one who selects what is good and firmly sticks to it.

（肖莉莉 译）

42 【原文】博学之，审问之，慎思之，明辨之，笃行之。

《中庸》

【今译】（对待学问）要广博地学习,详细的询问,慎重地思考,清楚地分辨,坚定不变地实行。

（肖莉莉 译）

【英译】When it comes to learning, one is expected to learn extensively, to inquire thoroughly, to reflect prudently, to discriminate clearly, and to practice steadfastly.

（肖莉莉 译）

43 【原文】有弗学,学之弗能,弗措也;有弗问,问之弗知,弗措也;有弗思,思之弗得,弗措也;有弗辨,辨之弗明,弗措也;有弗行,行之弗笃,弗措也。

《中庸》

【今译】人不学则已,一旦学了却学不会就不要放手;人不问则已,一旦问了却还不明白就不要止步;人不去思考则已,一旦思考了却还不明白就不要停止;人不辨别则已,一旦辨别了却还不能分辨明白就不要罢休;人不实践则已,一旦尽力去实践了却还不能奏效就不要中止。

（肖莉莉 译）

【英译】When you learn, do not let it go if you never learn; when you inquire, do not come to a halt if it is still dim for you; when you think, do not stop there if you fail to understand; when you discriminate, do not give up if there is no clear discrimination; when you practice, do not discontinue if you cannot succeed.

（肖莉莉 译）

44 【原文】人一能之,己百之;人十能之,己千之。

《中庸》

【今译】别人用一分的努力就做到的,我就用百倍的努力;别人用十分的努力就做到的,我就用千倍的努力。

（肖莉莉 译）

【英译】If one succeeds by one effort, I will employ a hundred. If one succeeds by ten efforts, I will employ a thousand.

（肖莉莉 译）

45 【原文】果能此道矣,虽愚必明,虽柔必强。

《中庸》

【今译】如果真能按这个方法去做,虽然愚昧也会变得聪明,虽然柔弱也会变得刚强。

（肖莉莉 译）

【英译】One who acts in this way, though dull, will become clever; though weak, will become strong.

（肖莉莉 译）

46 【原文】自诚明,谓之性;自明诚,谓之教。

《中庸》

【今译】由于真诚而能够明白道理,这就是先天的本性;由于明白道理而达到真诚,这就是后天的教育。

（肖莉莉 译）

【英译】Intelligence resulting from sincerity can be ascribed to nature; sincerity resulting from intelligence can be ascribed to nurture.

（肖莉莉 译）

47 【原文】诚则明矣，明则诚矣。

《中庸》

【今译】内心真诚就会明白道理，明白道理就会内心真诚。

（肖莉莉 译）

【英译】Where there is sincerity, there will be intelligence; where there is intelligence, there will be sincerity.

（肖莉莉 译）

48 【原文】唯天下至诚，为能尽其性；能尽其性，则能尽人之性；能尽人之性，则能尽物之性；能尽物之性，则可以赞天地之化育；可以赞天地之化育，则可以与天地参矣。

《中庸》

【今译】只有天下最真诚的人，才能充分发挥天赋的本性；能充分发挥天赋的本性，就能充分发挥天下众人的本性；能充分发挥天下众人的本性，就能充分发挥万物的本性；能充分发挥万物的本性，就可以帮助天地生育万物；能帮助天地生育万物，就可以与天地并立为三了。

（肖莉莉 译）

【英译】Only the most sincere people can give full play to their nature. When they can give full play to their nature, they can give full play to the nature of the multitude; when they can give full play to the nature of the multitude, they can give full play to the nature of things; when they can give full play to the nature of things, they can aid heaven and earth to produce and nourish things; when they can aid heaven and earth to produce and nourish things, they can unite heaven and earth to form a trinity.

（肖莉莉 译）

49 【原文】唯天下至诚为能化。

《中庸》

【今译】只有天下至诚的人才能化育万物。

（肖莉莉 译）

【英译】It is only one who owns the most complete sincerity that can produce and nourish all things.

（肖莉莉 译）

50 【原文】诚者自成也，而道自道也。

《中庸》

【今译】真诚是自我成就，而道是自我引导。

（肖莉莉 译）

【英译】Sincerity is a matter of self-completion, and its way is a matter of self-directing.

（肖莉莉 译）

51 【原文】诚者物之终始,不诚无物,是故君子诚之为贵。

《中庸》

【今译】真诚贯穿万物的终止和发端,没有真诚就没有万物,因此君子以真诚为贵。

(肖莉莉 译)

【英译】Sincerity is the beginning and end of all things. Without sincerity there would be nothing. Hence Junzi(a man of virtue) considers sincerity the soul of everything.

(肖莉莉 译)

52 【原文】成己,仁也;成物,知也。

《中庸》

【今译】成就自我是仁,成就万物是智。

(肖莉莉 译)

【英译】Self achievement is benevolence, and achievement of all things is wisdom.

(肖莉莉 译)

53 【原文】性之德也,合外内之道也,故时措之宜也。

《中庸》

【今译】仁和智是发自本性的品德,是将内心和外在结合在一起的准则,所以在任何时候施行都是适宜的。

(肖莉莉 译)

【英译】This is the virtue of nature which integrates ways of the internal and the external. Hence it is appropriate to carry out them from time to time.

(肖莉莉 译)

54 【原文】故至诚无息。

《中庸》

【今译】所以,最高境界的真诚永不停息。

(肖莉莉 译)

【英译】Hence the most complete sincerity is ceaseless.

(肖莉莉 译)

55 【原文】故曰:"苟不至德,至道不凝焉。"

《中庸》

【今译】所以说,如果没有最高的德行,就不能实行圣人之道。

(肖莉莉 译)

【英译】Hence it is said, "Only by perfect virtue can the highest moral be realized."

(肖莉莉 译)

56 【原文】万物并育而不相害,道并行而不相悖,小德川流,大德敦化。

《中庸》

【今译】万物同时生长而互不妨害,天地之道并行而互不违背。小德如江河一样川流不息,大德敦厚化育无穷无尽。

(肖莉莉 译)

【英译】All things grow together without impairing each other. The laws of nature run parallel without interfering with each other. Small virtues resemble the flowing of of rivers, while great virtues develop production and changes endlessly.

（肖莉莉 译）

（十六）《韩非子》
Han Feizi

1 【原文】夫严家无悍虏，而慈母有败子。

《韩非子·显学》

【今译】家教严格的家庭里不会出现凶悍不驯的莽夫，而慈爱的母亲的宽松管教下往往就会出现败家子。

（张龑真 译）

【英译】The strictly kept household sees no fierce men, but a compassionate mother has spoilt children.

（张龑真 译）

2 【原文】良药苦于口，而智者劝而饮之，知其入而已己疾也。

《韩非子·外储说左上》

【今译】虽然好的药物在口中很苦，但是明智的人不会因此拒绝服用，因为他知道这药可以治愈自己的疾病。

（张龑真 译）

【英译】Good medicine is bitter to the mouth, but intelligent people are willing to take them because they know the medicine will cure their diseases.

（张龑真 译）

3 【原文】思虑熟则得事理，得事理则必成功。

《韩非子·解老》

【今译】考虑周详，就会获得事理；获得事理，就必定会成功。

（张龑真 译）

【英译】By thinking thoughtfully, you can reach the truth of things; once you reach the truth of things, it will lead you to success.

（张龑真 译）

4 【原文】侈而惰者贫，而力而俭者富。

《韩非子·显学》

【今译】奢侈又懒惰的人会贫穷，如果努力劳作又勤俭节约的话就能富有。

（张龑真 译）

【英译】Extravagance and laziness invites poverty, while hard-working and thrift produces wealth.

（张龑真 译）

5 【原文】不吹毛而求疵。

《韩非子·说难》

【今译】不要吹毛求疵,故意挑剔别人的缺点。

(张燕真 译)

【英译】One should not be overcritical.

(张燕真 译)

6 【原文】家有常业,虽饥不饿;国有常法,虽危不亡。

《韩非子·饰邪》

【今译】家庭如果有固定的产业,即使闹饥荒,也不会挨饿;国家若能有健全的法制,即使遇到危难,也不会灭亡。

(张燕真 译)

【英译】A family that has a fixed industry will not starve, even when suffering from famine; the state that has a regular legal system will not perish, even when it is in crisis.

(张燕真 译)

7 【原文】安危在是非,不在于强弱;存亡在虚实,不在于众寡。

《韩非子·安危》

【今译】国家的安全或危险在于施政是否合乎事理的对与错,而不在于强大或弱小;国家的存在或灭亡在于国力的空虚或充实,而不在于民众数量的多与寡。

(张燕真 译)

【英译】The security or danger of a country lies in whether its governance is in line with justice, not in its strength or weakness. The existence or destruction of a country lies in the emptiness or enrichment of its national strength, not in the number of its people.

(张燕真 译)

8 【原文】夫物之待饰而后行者,其质不美也。

《韩非子·解老》

【今译】如果物品要等到装饰过以后才流行,那么它的质地肯定不美。

(张燕真 译)

【英译】If things are not appreciated until they are decorated, their texture is certainly not beautiful.

(张燕真 译)

(十七)《吕氏春秋》
Spring and Autumn Annals of Lü Buwei

1 【原文】是故古之圣王未有不尊师者也。

《吕氏春秋·劝学》

【今译】因此,古代贤明的君主没有不尊重老师的。

(肖莉莉 译)

【英译】Hence virtuous and wise sovereigns of ancient times would never fail to respect their teachers.

(肖莉莉 译)

2 【原文】尊师则不论其贵贱贫富矣。

《吕氏春秋·劝学》

【今译】尊重老师就不会去计较他们的贵贱与贫富。

(肖莉莉 译)

【英译】One will respect teachers regardless of their status and wealth.

(肖莉莉 译)

3 【原文】故师之教也,不争轻重尊卑贫富,而争于道。

《吕氏春秋·劝学》

【今译】所以,老师对学生的教化,并不在于对学生的尊卑、贫富看轻或看重,而是看重他们是否能够接受理义。

(肖莉莉 译)

【英译】Hence when teachers instruct, they ignore factors such as whether their students are rich or poor, honorable or humble, but rather whether they can accept Dao(Confucian doctrines) or not.

(肖莉莉 译)

4 【原文】圣人生于疾学。不疾学而能为魁士名人者,未之尝有也。

《吕氏春秋·劝学》

【今译】圣人是在勤奋学习中产生的,从来没有过不勤奋学习就能成为贤人名士这种事。

(肖莉莉 译)

【英译】Every sage must be the product of assiduous learning. None can become an eminent, erudite celebrity without such learning.

(肖莉莉 译)

5 【原文】疾学在于尊师。

《吕氏春秋·劝学》

【今译】勤奋学习的关键就在于尊重老师。

(肖莉莉 译)

【英译】The key of assiduous learning lies in respecting teachers.

(肖莉莉 译)

6 【原文】师尊则言信矣,道论矣。

《吕氏春秋·劝学》

【今译】老师受到尊重,他的言语就会被人信从,他所传的道就会被传论。

(肖莉莉 译)

【英译】Only when teachers are honoured will his words be followed and his Dao

(Confucian doctrines) accepted.

（肖莉莉 译）

7 【原文】凡说者，兑之也，非说之也。

《吕氏春秋·劝学》

【今译】但凡施教，都要循循善诱地对学生教诲，而不是去取悦对方。

（肖莉莉 译）

【英译】Whenever one instructs, he ought to educate the learners with skill and patience instead of pleasing them.

（肖莉莉 译）

8 【原文】故师必胜理行义然后尊。

《吕氏春秋·劝学》

【今译】所以，老师一定要依循事理，推行道义，然后才能受到尊敬。

（肖莉莉 译）

【英译】Hence teachers will be honoured only when they stick to truth and practice morality.

（肖莉莉 译）

9 【原文】古之贤者与，其尊师若此，故师尽智竭道以教。

《吕氏春秋·劝学》

【今译】古代圣贤的人，他们对老师如此尊重，所以老师竭尽才智来教导他们。

（肖莉莉 译）

【英译】Virtuous men in ancient times honoured their teachers so much that their teachers would go all out to instruct them.

（肖莉莉 译）

10 【原文】故凡学，非能益也，达天性也。

《吕氏春秋·尊师》

【今译】所以，学习并非能够给人增加好处，而是使人通达天性。

（肖莉莉 译）

【英译】Hence learning can not benefit one a lot, but rather enable one to approach his inborn nature.

（肖莉莉 译）

11 【原文】能全天之所生而勿败之，是谓善学。

《吕氏春秋·尊师》

【今译】能够保全上天赋予的本性而不使它受到损害，这就叫作善于学习。

（肖莉莉 译）

【英译】The so-called "good at learning" is actually a matter of preserving the inborn nature to be free from impairment.

（肖莉莉 译）

12 【原文】凡学,必务进业,心则无营。

《吕氏春秋·尊师》

【今译】但凡学习,都务求使学业进步,使得心中没有疑惑。

(肖莉莉 译)

【英译】A desire for learning aims at promoting academic achievements and staying away from doubts and puzzlement.

(肖莉莉 译)

13 【原文】物固莫不有长,莫不有短。人亦然。

《吕氏春秋·用众》

【今译】事物本来都各有其长,各有所短。人也是这样。

(肖莉莉 译)

【英译】All things in the world have their own strengths and weaknesses, and this is true of people.

(肖莉莉 译)

14 【原文】故善学者,假人之长以补其短。

《吕氏春秋·用众》

【今译】所以,善于学习的人,能吸取别人的长处来弥补自己的短处。

(肖莉莉 译)

【英译】Hence those who are good at learning can learn from each other's strong points to make up for their own shortcomings.

(肖莉莉 译)

15 【原文】故假人者遂有天下。

《吕氏春秋·用众》

【今译】因此,善于博采众长的人就能够拥有天下。

(肖莉莉 译)

【英译】Therefore, those who are good at learning from the strengths of others have the world.

(肖莉莉 译)

二 两汉三国时期
The Han Dynasties and the Three Kingdoms Period

(一)《汉乐府》
Yue Fu Poems of the Han Dynasty

【原文】少壮不努力,老大徒伤悲。

《汉乐府·长歌行》

【今译】年少时如果不努力,年老时只会悲伤悔恨而已。

(肖莉莉 译)

【英译】If one does not work hard in youth, he will feel sad and regret in old age.

(肖莉莉 译)

(二)《韩诗外传》
Hanshi Waizhuan

1 【原文】学而不已,阖棺乃止。

《韩诗外传》

【今译】学习无止境,一直到盖棺为止。

(肖莉莉 译)

【英译】There is no end of learning till one's death.

(肖莉莉 译)

2 【原文】智如泉源,行可以为仪表者,人之师也。

《韩诗外传》

【今译】智慧像泉水一样永不枯竭,行为堪当别人学习的榜样,就可以成为别人的老师了。

(肖莉莉 译)

【英译】One whose wisdom is like endless spring water and conducts a good model for others to follow is qualified to be a teacher.

（肖莉莉 译）

(三)《淮南子》
Huainanzi

1 【原文】知人无务,不若愚而好学。

《淮南子·修务训》

【今译】聪明的人无所作为,倒不如笨拙之人勤奋好学。

（肖莉莉 译）

【英译】A smart one who idles about all day is no better than a clumsy one who is diligent.

（肖莉莉 译）

2 【原文】不贵尺之璧,而贵寸之阴。

《淮南子·原道训》

【今译】不珍爱盈尺的璧玉,而是珍惜每一寸光阴。

（肖莉莉 译）

【英译】It is an inch of time that one treasures instead of a foot long piece of jade.

（肖莉莉 译）

(四)《史记》
Records of the Grand Historian

1 【原文】陈涉太息曰:"嗟乎！燕雀安知鸿鹄之志哉！"

《史记·陈涉世家》

【今译】陈涉叹息道:"唉！燕子、麻雀怎知大雁、天鹅的志向呢！"

（肖莉莉 译）

【英译】Chen She said with a sigh, "How can a sparrow get to know a swan's ambition?"

（肖莉莉 译）

2 【原文】忠言逆耳利于行,毒药苦口利于病。

《史记·留侯世家》

【今译】忠直之言虽听起来让人难以接受,但却有利于端正行为举止；毒药尝着虽有苦味,但却有利于病情。

（肖莉莉 译）

【英译】Though it sounds unacceptable, earnest advice is beneficial to action;

though it tastes bitter, strong medicine is conducive to illness.

（肖莉莉 译）

3 【原文】桃李不言，下自成蹊。

《史记·李将军列传》

【今译】桃李虽不言语，但它的鲜花和果实让人们在树下来回走动，便成了一条小路。

（肖莉莉 译）

【英译】Although peach and plum trees are speechless, their blossoms and fruits attract people and give rise to trodden paths under them.

（肖莉莉 译）

（五）《大戴礼记》
Elder Dai's Book of Rites

【原文】不能则学，疑则问。

《大戴礼记·曾子制言上》

【今译】不会就要去学习，有疑问就要向他人请教。

（肖莉莉 译）

【英译】If you fail to do something, just learn it; if you have doubts about something, just consult others.

（肖莉莉 译）

（六）《说苑·建本》
Garden of Anecdotes

1 【原文】讯问者，智之本；思虑者，智之道也。

《说苑·建本》

【今译】讯问是智慧的根本，思虑是智慧的方法。

（肖莉莉 译）

【英译】Consultation is the root of wisdom, and contemplation is the way of wisdom.

（肖莉莉 译）

2 【原文】书犹药也，善读之可以医愚。

《说苑·建本》

【今译】书就像药一样，阅读得法，就可以医治愚蠢。

（肖莉莉 译）

【英译】Books are like medicine. Reading appropriately may cure foolishness.

（肖莉莉 译）

（七）《汉书》
History of the Han Dynasty

1 【原文】遗子黄金满籝,不如一经。

《汉书·韦贤传》

【今译】给儿女留下满筐的金子,倒不如让他们学会一部经书。

（肖莉莉 译）

【英译】Leaving a basketful of gold to one's children is ultimately no better than providing them Confucian classics to learn.

（肖莉莉 译）

2 【原文】水至清则无鱼,人至察则无徒。

《汉书·东方朔传》

【今译】水清到极点,鱼就无法生存,人太严苛就没有同伴。

（肖莉莉 译）

【英译】There will be no fish if the water is extremely clear. One will have no company if he is overcritical.

（肖莉莉 译）

（八）《潜夫论》
A Treatise on the Latent Man

1 【原文】学进于振而废于穷。

《潜夫论·赞学》

【今译】勤奋学业才会有长进,否则只有倒退。

（肖莉莉 译）

【英译】Learning flourishes with persistent effort and declines when neglected.

（肖莉莉 译）

2 【原文】大人不华,君子务实。

《潜夫论·叙录》

【今译】优秀的人力戒华而不实的虚浮之气,君子致力于实际。

（肖莉莉 译）

【英译】Outstanding person avoids to be ostentatious, and Junzi(a man of virtue) is committed to being realistic and practical.

（肖莉莉 译）

（九）《中论》
On Appropriateness

1 【原文】学者如登山焉，动而益高。

《中论·治学》

【今译】学习就像登山，越往上爬就越向高处。

（肖莉莉 译）

【英译】Learning is just like climbing mountain, and the climber ascends a height with each movement.

（肖莉莉 译）

2 【原文】学者，不患才之不赡，而患志之不立。

《中论·治学》

【今译】治学之人不担心自己的才能不够，而是担心是否确立了志向。

（肖莉莉 译）

【英译】Learners do not worry about a shortage of ability but rather a lack of ambition.

（肖莉莉 译）

3 【原文】导人必因其性，治水必因其势。

《中论·贵言》

【今译】教育别人要因势利导，治理水流要参照地势。

（肖莉莉 译）

【英译】Educate a person according to his nature, and tame rivers according to their surroundings.

（肖莉莉 译）

（十）《诸葛亮集·诫子书》
Collected Works of Zhuge Liang

1 【原文】夫君子之行，静以修身，俭以养德。非淡泊无以明志，非宁静无以致远。

《诸葛亮集·诫子书》

【今译】君子应该宁静恬淡来修养自身，勤俭节约以培养品德。对名利如果不淡然处之就不能明确自己的志向，不宁静恬淡就不能达到深远的境界。

（肖莉莉 译）

【英译】Junzi(a man of virtue) should achieve self-cultivation by keeping peace of mind, and develop morality by frugality. Only indifference to fame and wealth can make clear one' own ambition; and only tranquility can make one reach profound realm.

（肖莉莉 译）

2 【原文】非学无以广才,非志无以成学。

《诸葛亮集·诫子书》

【今译】不学习就不能增长才干,不明确志向就不能在学业上获得成就。

(肖莉莉 译)

【英译】One cannot develop talent without learning, and one cannot achieve academic success without ambition.

(肖莉莉 译)

(十一)《万机论》
On State Affairs

【原文】学如牛毛,成如麟角。

《万机论》

【今译】学的人很多,但学成的人却极少。

(肖莉莉 译)

【英译】Learners are countless, while the accomplished are rare.

(肖莉莉 译)

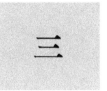

魏晋南北朝时期
Period of Wei, Jin, Southern and Northern Dynasties

（一）《三国志》
History of the Three Kingdoms

【原文】读书百遍，而义自见。

《三国志·魏书·王肃传》

【今译】读书上百遍，书中的意思自然显现。

（肖莉莉 译）

【英译】Once a book is read a hundred times, its meaning will come to be known naturally.

（肖莉莉 译）

（二）陶渊明诗文
Poems & Writings of Tao Yuanming

1 【原文】盛年不复来，一日难再晨。及时当勉励，岁月不待人。

《杂诗（之一）》

【今译】美好的年华一旦逝去便不复还，一日之中没有两次清晨。趁着大好时光应当自我勉励，光阴流逝，并不等待人。

（肖莉莉 译）

【英译】Once gone, the prime of life will not come back again;
A second dawn will not occur again in a single day.
Hold fast the time and encourage one another;
Since time and tide wait for no man.

（肖莉莉 译）

2 【原文】好读书，不求甚解。

《五柳先生传》

【今译】喜好读书，但求通达大意，不拘泥于字里行间细致的解释。

（肖莉莉 译）

【英译】He has profound affection for reading, but reads for a general idea instead of a thorough understanding.

（肖莉莉 译）

（三）《世说新语》
A New Account of Tales of the World

1 【原文】吾家君譬如桂树生泰山之阿，上有万仞之高，下有不测之深；上为甘露所沾，下为渊泉所润。

《世说新语·德行第一》

【今译】我父亲好比生在泰山角落的一棵桂树，上有万丈高峰，下有深不可测的深渊，上受雨露浇灌，下受深泉滋润。

（张巽真 译）

【英译】My father is like a cassia tree growing on the hillside of Mount Tai. It's ten thousand feet high above, and it's immeasurable deep below. It is watered by rain and dew, and moistened by deep spring.

（张巽真 译）

2 【原文】在家思孝，事君思忠，朋友思信。

《世说新语·言语第二》

【今译】在家中要想着孝敬父母，侍奉君主要忠心不二，和朋友相处要讲信义。

（张巽真 译）

【英译】We should be filial to our parents at home, loyal to the king in service, and faithful to our friends.

（张巽真 译）

3 【原文】蒲柳之姿，望秋而落；松柏之质，经霜弥茂。

《世说新语·言语第二》

【今译】蒲苇和柳树的姿色，到了秋天就凋落了；松树和柏树的品性，经过冰霜的摧残反而更加坚定。

（张巽真 译）

【英译】The beauty of pampasgrass and willow withers in autumn, while the nature of pine and cypress is strengthened in ice and frost.

（张巽真 译）

4 【原文】宁为兰摧玉折，不作萧敷艾荣。

《世说新语·言语第二》

【今译】宁可做被摧残的香兰、被打碎的美玉,也不做生长茂盛开花的艾蒿。

(张羹真 译)

【英译】I'd rather be an orchid plucked, or jade broken, than artemisia in profusion, or mugwort in full bloom. (A man of high morality) would rather be a ruined orchid, a broken jade, than a prosperous wormwood.

(张羹真 译)

5 【原文】人自量,固为难!

《世说新语·方正第五》

【今译】人能做到正确估量自己,真是不容易啊!

(张羹真 译)

【英译】It's not easy for people to evaluate themselves correctly!

(张羹真 译)

6 【原文】肃肃如入廊庙中,不修敬而人自敬。

《世说新语·赏誉第八》

【今译】好比到了宗庙或朝廷一样严肃而恭敬,不需要别人致敬却自然而然能让人产生敬意。

(张羹真 译)

【英译】He is solemn and revered, as if entering a temple or a court. He doesn't need other people to bow and salute, but it can naturally make people respectful.

(张羹真 译)

7 【原文】森森如千丈松,虽磊砢有节目,施之大厦,有栋梁之用。

《世说新语·赏誉第八》

【今译】好像高耸入云的千丈青松,虽然圪节累累,可是用它来盖高楼大厦,还是可以用作栋梁之材。

(张羹真 译)

【英译】It's like a gnarled pine tree growing to a height of a thousand zhang with many knots, which can still be used as pillars to build tall buildings.

(张羹真 译)

8 【原文】君贤臣忠,国之盛也;父慈子孝,家之盛也。

《世说新语·规箴第十》

【今译】君主贤能、臣子忠贞,国就能兴盛;父亲慈爱、儿子孝顺,家就能兴盛。

(张羹真 译)

【英译】The country will prosper when the king is virtuous and his ministers are loyal; the family will prosper when the father is kind and the son is filial.

(张羹真 译)

9 【原文】桑榆之光,理无远照,但愿朝阳之晖,与时并明耳。

《世说新语·规箴第十》

【今译】人的晚年就像夕阳的光辉,没有多少照耀的时刻了;但愿少年人能像早晨的太阳,随早晨以后的时光一起散发光芒。

(张橅真 译)

【英译】Twilight years of life is like the light of the setting sun, and there is not much time left to shine. I only pray that the young people will become brighter with passage of time, just as the light of the morning.

(张橅真 译)

10 【原文】欲自修改而年已蹉跎,终无所成。

《世说新语·自新第十五》

【今译】自己想要修身改错,但是年岁已太大了,终究不能有什么成就。

(张橅真 译)

【英译】I've wanted to improve myself, but the years have already slipped by, and I am too old to achieve anything.

(张橅真 译)

11 【原文】为子则孝,为臣则忠。

《世说新语·贤媛第十九》

【今译】作为儿子应当孝顺,作为人臣应当忠诚。

(张橅真 译)

【英译】We should be filial as a son and loyal as a minister.

(张橅真 译)

(四)《文心雕龙》
The Literary Mind and the Carving of Dragons

1 【原文】志足而言文,情信而辞巧。

《文心雕龙·征圣》

【今译】思想内容要充实,语言就会有文采;感情要真实,文辞也会美好。

(张橅真 译)

【英译】If the thought is substantial, the language will be elegant; if the feelings are true, the language will be beautiful.

(张橅真 译)

2 【原文】夫文以行立,行以文传,四教所先,符采相济。

《文心雕龙·宗经》

【今译】文章靠作者的品行才能立足,作者的品行靠文章才能传布。孔子在"四教(文辞、德行、忠诚、信义)"中,将文辞放在了首位,正如玉石必须有精致的花纹一样相济相成,文辞也必须与德行、忠诚、信义三者互相结合。

(张橅真 译)

【英译】Writing is sustained by virtue; virtue is passed down in writing. Writing and virtue together complement conscientiousness and truthfulness in the four Confucian teachings.

(杨国斌,2003)³³

3 【原文】酌奇而不失其(真)贞,玩华而不坠其实。

《文心雕龙·辨骚》

【今译】选取奇伟的内容但是不失掉它的真实,讲究华丽雕琢但不失掉它的实质。

(张羿真 译)

【英译】Choose gorgeous ideas on the premise of not losing the truth, and appreciate colorful things on the premise of not losing the essence.

(张羿真 译)

4 【原文】诗者,持也,持人情性。

《文心雕龙·明诗》

【今译】"诗"的含义是扶持,诗就是用来扶持人的情性的。

(张羿真 译)

【英译】The nature of "poetry" is "discipline", and poetry is the discipline of human nature.

(张羿真 译)

5 【原文】文以辨洁为能,不以繁缛为巧;
事以明核为美,不以深隐为奇。

《文心雕龙·议对》

【今译】文章以说理明晰、行文简洁为高明,不以冗长繁复为巧妙;文中所阐述的事实和道理以明白准确为美好,不以艰深隐晦、难于理解为奇特。

(张羿真 译)

【英译】An excellent article should be clear in reasoning and concise in writing. Extravagantly ornate diction can't make the article appear ingenious; a good argument in the article should be lucid and accurate, not ambiguous and obscure.

(张羿真 译)

6 【原文】积学以储宝,酌理以富才。

《文心雕龙·神思》

【今译】积累学识来储存珍宝,斟酌辨析事理来丰富增长才学。

(张羿真 译)

【英译】To accumulate knowledge is to accumulate wealth, and to judge and reason is to enrich talent.

(张羿真 译)

7 【原文】气以实志,志以定言,吐纳英华,莫非情性。

《文心雕龙·体性》

【今译】培养气质以充实人的情志,充实情志来确定文章的语言;文章能否写得精美,无不来自人的情性。

(张羿真 译)

【英译】Vitality nourishes thought and thought shapes language. The flowers and fruits of words grow from natural endowment.

（张奚真 译）

8 【原文】水性虚而沦漪结，木体实而花萼振。

《文心雕龙·情采》

【今译】由于水性虚柔，才有波纹荡漾；由于树体坚实，才有花朵开放。

（张奚真 译）

【英译】The ripples are caused by the flow of water, and the flowers bloom because the plants are solid.

（张奚真 译）

9 【原文】夫铅黛所以饰容，而盼倩生于淑姿；文采所以饰言，而辩丽本于情性。

《文心雕龙·情采》

【今译】铅粉和黛石是用来修饰容颜的，但是流转的眼波是生在美好的姿容上的；文采是用来修饰言辞的，但是哲理的思辨和辞藻的华丽，是来源于至情至性的情感。

（张奚真 译）

【英译】Powder and eyebrow pencil can add to female beauty, but real charm comes from natural looks. Language can be modified by literary talent, but real force and beauty spring from real feelings deep inside the heart.

（张奚真 译）

10 【原文】桃李不言而成蹊，有实存也。

《文心雕龙·情采》

【今译】桃树和李树不会说话，但是人会在树下踩出路来，只是因为它们会结出甜美的果实。

（张奚真 译）

【英译】Peach and plum trees do not talk, but path is formed beneath because of their sweet fruits.

（张奚真 译）

11 【原文】凡操千曲而后晓声，观千剑而后识器。

《文心雕龙·知音》

【今译】只有弹奏过千百支乐曲之后才能懂得音乐；观察过千百柄宝剑之后才懂得如何识别武器。

（张奚真 译）

【英译】Only by playing thousands of tunes can we understand music; only by observing thousands of swords can we understand how to identify good weapons.

（张奚真 译）

(五)《颜氏家训》
Admonition for the Yan Clan

1 【原文】夫圣贤之书,教人诚孝,慎言检迹,立身扬名,亦已备矣。

《颜氏家训·序致》

【今译】古代圣贤的著述,教诲人们要忠诚孝顺,说话谨慎,行为庄重,要建立高尚的人格,并且声名远扬,这些道理他们已经说得很完备了。

(张冀真 译)

【英译】The works of ancient sages have taught people to be loyal and filial, to advocate careful speech and prudent behavior, and to attain integrity and reputation. What they said is very comprehensive.

(张冀真 译)

2 【原文】同言而信,信其所亲;同命而行,行其所服。

《颜氏家训·序致》

【今译】同样的话语有些人会相信,是因为人们愿意相信与自己关系亲密的人所说的话;同样的指令有些人会执行,是因为人们愿意接受自己所敬佩的人发出的指令。

(张冀真 译)

【英译】Advices are more likely to be followed when they come from a loved one; commands are more willingly to be carried out when they come from an authority.

(张冀真 译)

3 【原文】积财千万,不如薄技在身。

《颜氏家训·勉学》

【今译】积累的财富有千千万,都不如身上有点小技能。

(张冀真 译)

【英译】The accumulated wealth is not as good as a practical skill.

(张冀真 译)

4 【原文】夫学者所以求益耳。

《颜氏家训·勉学》

【今译】人们学习是为了求取更多收获和提高。

(张冀真 译)

【英译】People study so that they can improve themselves.

(张冀真 译)

5 【原文】夫学者,犹种树也,春玩其华,秋登其实。

《颜氏家训·勉学》

【今译】学习就像是种植树木一样,春天可以观赏它的花朵,秋天可以摘取它的果实。

(张冀真 译)

【英译】Learning is like planting fruit trees: one takes delight in learning and writing much the same as one enjoys the blossoms in spring; one reaps the benefit of good conduct much the same as one picks the fruit in autumn.

(宗福常，2004)⁸⁴

6 【原文】人有坎壈，失于盛年，犹当晚学，不可自弃。

《颜氏家训·勉学》

【今译】人有困穷不得志的时候，即使失去了青壮年学习的大好时光，也应当在晚年的时候抓紧学习，不可自暴自弃。

(张篪真 译)

【英译】If a person is deprived of the right of receiving education in the hard times, he should make good use of the rest of his life to learn and never give up.

(张篪真 译)

7 【原文】夫所以读书学问，本欲开心明目，利于行耳。

《颜氏家训·勉学》

【今译】人们之所以要读书做学问，本意是为了使心胸开阔、眼睛明亮，有利于更好地做事情。

(张篪真 译)

【英译】The reason why people want to read and learn is to make their minds open and their eyes bright, which is conductive to doing things better.

(张篪真 译)

8 【原文】人生小幼，精神专利，长成已后，思虑散逸，固须早教，勿失机也。

《颜氏家训·勉学》

【今译】人在幼年的时候，注意力高，容易专心，长大成人后，精神涣散，难以专心，所以需要在幼年的时候对人进行教育，不要错过这个大好时机。

(张篪真 译)

【英译】Education for young people must begin at an early age, when they are most attentive and receptive; it would be too late for them to start in adulthood, when they will find it difficult to concentrate on their studies. It would be a pity that the young people miss the great time of study.

(张篪真 译)

9 【原文】观天下书未遍，不得妄下雌黄。

《颜氏家训·勉学》

【今译】没有看遍古今中外的书，就不能轻易说三道四、信口雌黄。

(张篪真 译)

【英译】Don't say anything easily if you haven't read enough books about it.

(张篪真 译)

10 【原文】自古明王圣帝，犹须勤学，况凡庶乎！

《颜氏家训·勉学》

【今译】从古以来,圣明贤德的帝王还需要勤奋学习,何况是普通百姓呢!

(张奚真 译)

【英译】Down the ages, wise emperors still need to be diligent in learning, let alone ordinary people.

(张奚真 译)

11 【原文】若能常保数百卷书,千载终不为小人也。

《颜氏家训·勉学》

【今译】如果能保持有几百卷书,就是再过一千年,也不会沦为贫贱之人。

(张奚真 译)

【英译】If one can keep a few thousand books, even after another thousand years, he/she will not be reduced to an ordinary person.

(张奚真 译)

12 【原文】幼而学者,如日出之光;老而学者,如秉烛夜行,犹贤乎瞑目而无见者也。

《颜氏家训·勉学》

【今译】幼年学习的人像太阳刚升起的光芒;老年学习的人,像夜里走路拿着蜡烛,总比闭上眼睛什么也看不见要好。

(张奚真 译)

【英译】To begin studying from an early age is like the rising sun, shining brightly; to begin studying from an old age is like walking with candle light at night, which is better than closing your eyes and seeing nothing.

(张奚真 译)

13 【原文】学之所知,施无不达。世人读书者,但能言之,不能行之。

《颜氏家训·勉学》

【今译】从学习中所获取的知识,在哪里都可以运用。然而现在的读书人,只知空谈,不能行动。

(张奚真 译)

【英译】Knowledge acquired from learning can be used everywhere. However nowadays, scholars only indulge in empty talk but cannot put into practice.

(刘士聪、谷启楠英译)[225]

14 【原文】凡为文章,犹人乘骐骥,虽有逸气,当以衔勒制之。

《颜氏家训·文章》

【今译】作文章就好比是人骑千里马,虽然马很骏逸奔放,也还是得用衔勒来控制它。

(张奚真 译)

【英译】Writing may be compared to riding. The horse, though mettlesome, must be checked with a bridle.

(尹邦彦、尹海波,2009)[84]

15 【原文】文章当以理致为心肾,气调为筋骨,事义为皮肤,华丽为冠冕。

《颜氏家训·文章》

【今译】写文章要将义理情致作为文章的心肾,把气韵格调作为筋骨,把运用恰当的典故作为皮肤,把华丽辞藻作为冠冕。

(张燮真 译)

【英译】For writing, idea is the heart; feeling, the kidneys; spirit and style, the bones; allusions and references, the skin; and elaborate diction, the adornment.

(宗福常,2004)[177]

16 【原文】不修身而求令名于世者,犹貌甚恶而责妍影于镜也。

《颜氏家训·名实》

【今译】不修正自身,却想要在世上有美好的名声,就像是相貌丑陋的人却责怪镜子不能照出自己美丽的影像一样。

(张燮真 译)

【英译】Anyone who wishes to achieve a good reputation but refuses to improve himself is like an ugly person blaming the mirror for not reflecting a perfect image.

(张燮真 译)

17 【原文】士君子之处世,贵能有益于物耳。不徒高谈虚论,左琴右书,以费人君禄位也。

《颜氏家训·涉务》

【今译】士大夫君子处身立世,贵在能有益于社会万物,不能只知高谈阔论、抚琴读书,白白浪费国家官位俸禄。

(张燮真 译)

【英译】The value of a scholar lies in the benefits he can bring to the public. He should not indulge in empty talk of hobbies like calligraphy, or playing *guzheng* while holding a public post and receiving government wages.

(张燮真 译)

18 【原文】多为少善,不如执一。

《颜氏家训·省事》

【今译】做的事情很多,但能做好的很少,还不如专心做好一件事。

(张燮真 译)

【英译】It's better to concentrate on one thing and do it well instead of attempting many things with little effect.

(张燮真 译)

19 【原文】与善人居,如入芝兰之室,久而自芳也;与恶人居,如入鲍鱼之肆,久而自臭也。

《颜氏家训·慕贤》

【今译】和品德高尚的人交往,就像进入摆放着芳香兰花的房间,时间久了,自然会散发出芳香;和品德恶劣的人交往,就像进入卖腌鱼的店铺,时间久了,自身便会散发出腥臭。

(张燮真 译)

【英译】A person in good company becomes scented, as if living in a room of fragrant orchids, whereas a person in bad company turns malodorous, as if staying long in a market of salted fish.

(宗福常，2004)[176]

20 【原文】学如牛毛，成如麟角。

《颜氏家训·养生》

【今译】学习的人多如牛毛，而学有成就的人却凤毛麟角。

(张奠真 译)

【英译】Many people study, but few people succeed.

(张奠真 译)

四 唐宋时期
Period of the Tang and Song Dynasties

（一）王之涣 Wang Zhihuan

【原文】欲穷千里目，更上一层楼。

《登鹳雀楼》

【今译】若想尽览风景，那就要登上更高的一层城楼。

（肖莉莉 译）

【英译】To view a thousand miles away, one needs to take one more storey up.

（肖莉莉 译）

（二）李白 Li Bai

1 【原文】天生我材必有用，千金散尽还复来。

《将进酒》

【今译】每个人只要生下来就必有用处，千两黄金一散而尽还能够再得到。

（肖莉莉 译）

【英译】Talents that Heaven has bestowed us will be of use. A thousand gold scattered to the wind will come back again.

（肖莉莉 译）

2 【原文】长风破浪会有时，直挂云帆济沧海。

《行路难》

【今译】总会有一天，我能乘长风破万里浪；高高挂起云帆，在沧海中勇往直前。

（张燮真 译）

【英译】The time will come for me to ride the wind and cleave the waves, when I hoist the sails to cross the sea.

（张燮真 译）

3 【原文】仰天大笑出门去,我辈岂是蓬蒿人。

《南陵别儿童入京》

【今译】我仰起头高声大笑地走出门去,像我这样的人,岂能永远埋没、甘心做个毫无用处之人吗?

(张燮真 译)

【英译】I lean back roaring with laughter and walk out of the door. Can a person like me be buried forever and willing to be useless?

(张燮真 译)

4 【原文】安能摧眉折腰事权贵,使我不得开心颜。

《梦游天姥吟留别》

【今译】怎么能低眉弯腰、巴结奉承去侍奉那些权贵之人,让我自己一点都不能开心快乐。

(张燮真 译)

【英译】How can I bend my knees and bow to serve those powerful people? I can't be happy at all in that way.

(张燮真 译)

5 【原文】宣父犹能畏后生,丈夫未可轻年少。

《上李邕》

【今译】连孔圣人都曾说过"后生可畏",你们这些老夫子实在不该轻视少年人!

(张燮真 译)

【英译】Even Confucius once said that "an after-born should be feared". You old men should not despise the young!

(张燮真 译)

6 【原文】土扶可城墙,积德为厚地。

《君道曲》

【今译】泥土积累多了,可以筑成城墙;美德积累多了,可以成为安身立命的基础。

(张燮真 译)

【英译】With more accumulated soil, you can build walls; with more accumulated virtues you can build the foundation for your life.

(张燮真 译)

(三) 杜甫 *Du Fu*

1 【原文】读书破万卷,下笔如有神。

《奉赠韦左丞丈二十二韵》

【今译】胸罗万卷,下笔犹如神助。

(肖莉莉 译)

【英译】When you have read thousands of books, you can write with a gifted pen.

(肖莉莉 译)

2 【原文】安得广厦千万间,大庇天下寒士俱欢颜!

《茅屋为秋风所破歌》

【今译】如何能得到千万间宽敞高大的房子？庇护天下贫寒的人,使他们能开颜欢笑!

(张奚真 译)

【英译】Where can I get thousands of big broad shelters with huge roofs that all the world's poor people can share with smiling faces?

(张奚真 译)

3 【原文】少壮能几时？鬓发各已苍!

《赠卫八处士》

【今译】年少力壮能有多少时日啊？你我都已是两鬓斑白,苍苍暮年了。

(张奚真 译)

【英译】How long can youth and strength maintain? We are both already old and gray.

(张奚真 译)

4 【原文】富贵必从勤苦得,男儿须读五车书。

《柏学士茅屋》

【今译】富贵腾达必定从勤苦努力中得到,男儿想有所成就,必须博览群书、学富五车。

(张奚真 译)

【英译】Wealth must come from hard work. If a man wants to make achievements, he must read a lot and learn a lot.

(张奚真 译)

5 【原文】读书难字过,对酒满壶频。

《漫成二首》

【今译】读书不求甚解,难读之字不考究任其读过；酣畅淋漓地饮酒,借酒怡情。

(张奚真 译)

【英译】Read without investigating the difficult parts or seeking deep understanding, but just enjoy the books while drinking wine fully and delightfully.

(张奚真 译)

6 【原文】竹斋烧药灶,花屿读书床。

《寄彭州高三十五使君适虢州岑二十七长史参三十韵》

【今译】竹子斋屋里立着熬煮汤药的炉灶,水旁开着花的小山头是悠闲读书的好地方。

(张奚真 译)

【英译】The stove set up in the bamboo house is boiling herbs, and the small island with flowers is a good place for reading.

(张奚真 译)

7 【原文】负米力葵外,读书秋树根。卜邻惭近舍,训子学谁门。

《孟氏》

【今译】孟氏家的兄弟背着米和野菜到外面,秋天在树下读书。近邻们都感到惭愧,训斥孩子该向谁学习?

(张燮真 译)

【英译】The Meng brothers often carry rice and wild vegetables outside, and read books under the trees in autumn. The neighbors feel ashamed to see that, and scold the children, asking them who they should learn from?

(张燮真 译)

8 【原文】丹青不知老将至,富贵于我如浮云。

《丹青引赠曹将军霸》

【今译】毕生潜心绘画竟然不知老之将至,荣华富贵我来说,就像空中浮云一样淡薄。

(张燮真 译)

【英译】I've devoted my whole life to painting without knowing the insidious approach of old age. To me, fame and wealth are like floating clouds of nothingness.

(张燮真 译)

(四) 孟郊 Meng Jiao

1 【原文】谁言寸草心,报得三春晖?

《游子吟》

【今译】谁能说子女像小草那样的孝心,能够报答得了春晖般的慈母恩情呢?

(肖莉莉 译)

【英译】The gratitude of petty grass can never repay the grace of the spring sunshine.

(肖莉莉 译)

2 【原文】青春须早为,岂能长少年!

《劝学》

【今译】青春年少时学习须趁早,一个人难道能够永远都是"少年"吗?

(肖莉莉 译)

【英译】One should learn at an early age, since youth does not last long.

(肖莉莉 译)

3 【原文】夜学晓未休,苦吟神鬼愁。

《夜感自遣》

【今译】夜里学习一直到拂晓还没有停歇,苦心钻研吟诗连鬼神都无可奈何。

(张燮真 译)

【英译】I learn at night and wouldn't rest till dawn. I study poetry so hard that even gods and ghosts are worried.

（张龑真 译）

4 【原文】人学始知道，不学非自然。

《劝学》

【今译】人只有读书学习才能懂得"道"；如果不学习就不能按照"道"来自然行事。

（张龑真 译）

【英译】Only by reading and learning can people understand the rules of nature; if they don't study, they can't act accordingly.

（张龑真 译）

5 【原文】登山须正路，饮水须直流。

《送丹霞子阮芳颜上人归山》

【今译】登山的时候要走正路，喝水的时候要饮直流。

（张龑真 译）

【英译】One should take the right path when climbing, and drink fresh water when drinking.

（张龑真 译）

6 【原文】镜破不改光，兰死不改香。

《赠别崔纯亮》

【今译】镜子就算破了也可以发光，兰花就算凋零了也依旧芳香。

（张龑真 译）

【英译】Broken mirror can still reflect light, while the withered orchid does not change fragrance.

（张龑真 译）

（五）杜荀鹤 *Du Xunhe*

1 【原文】鬓白只应秋炼句，眼昏多为夜抄书。

《闲居书事》

【今译】双鬓斑白只是因为秋天赋诗推敲提炼词句，两眼昏花多是因为夜里誊抄诗书。

（张龑真 译）

【英译】The reason why my temples are white is that the words and sentences of poems are pondered over and over again. The reason why my eyes are dim is that I transcribe poems and books at night.

（张龑真 译）

2 【原文】昼短夜长须强学，学成贫亦胜他贫。

《喜从弟雪中远至有作》

【今译】冬天白天短黑夜长，人们应更加刻苦学习，学有所成哪怕虽然生活依旧贫困，但是也比其他精神上的贫困要好很多。

（张龑真 译）

【英译】People should be diligent in learning even if the days are short and the nights are long. Even if one still lives in poverty, it is much better than living in spiritual poverty.

（张奠真 译）

3 【原文】百年能几日，忍不惜光阴。

《赠李蒙叟》

【今译】一百年又能有多久？怎么忍心不珍惜光阴。

（张奠真 译）

【英译】How long can one hundred years last? How can one bear not to cherish time?

（张奠真 译）

4 【原文】少年辛苦终身事，莫向光阴惰寸功。

《题弟侄书堂》

【今译】年轻时候的努力是有益终身的大事，对着匆匆逝去的光阴，不要丝毫放松自己的努力。

（张奠真 译）

【英译】The effort in your youth will benefit yourself lifelong. Don't slacken your efforts as time goes by.

（张奠真 译）

5 【原文】共莫更初志，俱期立后名。

《寄李溥》

【今译】我们不要改变初心，期待能在青史上留名。

（张奠真 译）

【英译】We should remain true to our original aspiration, looking forward that history (will) hand down our names.

（张奠真 译）

6 【原文】男儿出门志，不独为谋身。

《秋宿山馆》

【今译】男儿在外闯荡的志向，不应该只为自己的温饱牟利。

（张奠真 译）

【英译】A man's ambition to roam outside should not be all about himself.

（张奠真 译）

（六）陆游 *Lu You*

1 【原文】纸上得来终觉浅，绝知此事要躬行。

《冬夜读书示子聿八首》

【今译】从书本上得来的知识到底流于肤浅，要想真正融会贯通，终究还是要把所学付诸实践。

（肖莉莉 译）

【英译】What one gains from books tends to be superficial. To really digest what one has learned, the only way is to put it into practice.

（肖莉莉 译）

2 【原文】宦途至老无余俸,贫悴还如筮仕初。
赖有一筹胜富贵,小儿读遍旧藏书。

《冬夜读书示子聿八首》

【今译】当官一辈子到老了也没有积攒下来多余的俸禄,贫穷得就像是当初刚刚上任时一样。
幸好还有一个好处能胜过大富大贵,那就是小孩子能够读遍旧时收藏的诗书。

（张巽真 译）

【英译】I have no savings in my life as an official.
Now I am as poor as when I just took the office.
The only advantage is that children can read many old books
Which is more valuable than wealth.

（张巽真 译）

3 【原文】位卑未敢忘忧国,事定犹须待阖棺。

《病起书怀二首》

【今译】虽然职位低微但却从来不敢忘记忧虑国事,一个人的是非功过还要等到盖棺方能定论。

（张巽真 译）

【英译】Although my position is low, I never dare to forget to worry about my country. A man's merits and demerits will not be determined until his death.

（张巽真 译）

4 【原文】古人学问无遗力,少壮工夫老始成。

《冬夜读书示子聿八首》

【今译】古人做学问是不遗余力的,从年轻时开始下工夫往往要到老年才取得成就。

（张巽真 译）

【英译】The ancients spared no effort in learning. However, they began to work hard when they were young, yet they often didn't make achievements until they were old.

（张巽真 译）

5 【原文】丈夫贵不挠,成败何足论。

《入瞿唐登白帝庙》

【今译】大丈夫最难能可贵的就是不屈不挠的精神,至于成功还是失败,哪里还值得论道呢?

（张巽真 译）

【英译】The most precious thing about a great man is his indomitable spirit. As for success or failure, is it worth discussing?

（张巽真 译）

6 【原文】归志宁无五亩园,读书本意在元元。
　　　　灯前目力虽非昔,犹课蝇头二万言。

《读书二首之二》

　　【今译】归隐的志向就算没有那五亩田地也依然如故,读书的本意在于为了天下百姓。灯下读书眼力虽然已经大不如前,但还是读完了两万多蝇头小字的书。

（张奭真 译）

　　【英译】The will of returning to my hometown and living in seclusion after retirement remains the same even if there is not much land. The purpose of studying is to serve the people. Although my eyes are not as good as before when I read under the light, I have finished reading more than 20,000 small words of the book.

（张奭真 译）

7 【原文】六十余年妄学诗,功夫深处独心知。
　　　　夜来一笑寒灯下,始是金丹换骨时。

《夜吟》

　　【今译】六十多年来我胡乱学诗,作诗的功夫有多深只有我自己内心知道。夜里独坐在寒灯下,不由发出会心的一笑时,才是达到了像服下金丹妙药脱胎换骨一样的境界。

（张奭真 译）

　　【英译】For more than 60 years, I have been learning poetry casually, and only I know the depth of my poetic skills. Sitting alone in the cold light at night, with a knowing smile, my inspiration is like taking the pill of immortality.

（张奭真 译）

8 【原文】看尽人间兴废事,不曾富贵不曾穷。

《一壶歌》

　　【今译】看遍了人世间的兴衰起伏,谁也不曾大富大贵,也没有谁曾贫穷。

（张奭真 译）

　　【英译】After experiencing the ups and downs of the world, I know that no one has ever been rich or poor.

（张奭真 译）

（七）吴兢 *Wu Jing*

　　【原文】以铜为镜,可以正衣冠;以古为镜,可以见兴替;以人为镜,可以知得失。

吴兢《贞观政要·任贤》

　　【今译】用铜来做镜子,可以用来端正衣冠;用古史做镜子,可以从中发现盛衰交替;用人做镜子,可以知道自己的得失。

（肖莉莉 译）

　　【英译】With copper as a mirror, one can regulate his attires; with history as a mirror, one can find prosperity and decline of a state; with men as a mirror, one can know his gains and losses.

（肖莉莉 译）

（八）韩愈 Han Yu

1 【原文】师者，所以传道受业解惑也。

《师说》

【今译】教师的职责是传授道理、讲授学业、解答疑惑。

（肖莉莉 译）

【英译】A teacher is one who propagates the doctrine, imparts knowledge, and removes doubts.

（肖莉莉 译）

2 【原文】业精于勤，荒于嬉；行成于思，毁于随。

《进学解》

【今译】学业由于勤奋而精进，由于嬉戏而荒废；做事情成功是因为能够独立思考，由于因循随俗而毁损。

（肖莉莉 译）

【英译】Learning can be heightened through diligence and ruined by idleness. Morality can be achieved by an independent mind and ruined by following the beaten track.

（肖莉莉 译）

（九）刘禹锡 Liu Yuxi

【原文】山不在高，有仙则名。水不在深，有龙则灵。

《陋室铭》

【今译】山不在于高，有了神仙就有了名气。水不在于深，有了龙就有了灵气。

（肖莉莉 译）

【英译】Though not high, a mountain can be famous with an immortal in it; though not deep, a river can be holy with a dragon in it.

（肖莉莉 译）

（十）严羽 Yan Yu

【原文】学其上，仅得其中；学其中，斯为下矣。

《沧浪诗话·诗辨》

【今译】向上等的学习,可能只能得到中等的效果;向中等的学习,就只能达到下等水平。

(肖莉莉 译)

【英译】One can only get a medium level if a high standard is set; one can only get a low level if a medium standard is set.

(肖莉莉 译)

(十一) 范仲淹 Fan Zhongyan

【原文】先天下之忧而忧,后天下之乐而乐。

《岳阳楼记》

【今译】在天下人忧愁之前先忧愁,在天下人享乐之后才享乐。

(肖莉莉 译)

【英译】One should be the first to worry about state affairs and the last to enjoy comforts.

(肖莉莉 译)

(十二) 司马光 Sima Guang

【原文】学者贵于行之,而不贵于知之。

《答孔文仲司户书》

【今译】求学之人重要的是将学到的知识付诸实践,而不仅仅是了解、知道它。

(肖莉莉 译)

【英译】When it comes to learning, practice is far more valuable than just knowing it.

(肖莉莉 译)

(十三) 张载 Zhang Zai

【原文】为天地立心,为生民立道,为往圣继绝学,为万世开太平。

《张子全书·性理拾遗》

【今译】为天地确立生生之心,为百姓确立立命之本,为历代圣贤延续不朽学说,给千秋万代开创太平盛世的局面。

(张夔真 译)

【英译】To ordain conscience for Heaven and Earth, to secure life and fortune for the people, to continue lost teachings for past sages, and establish peace for all future generations.

(佚名 译)

2 【原文】人若志趣不远,心不在焉,虽学无成。

《张子全书·经学理窟·义理篇》

【今译】志向和情趣不远大,不能专心致志,即便是学了也不会有什么成就。

(张夔真 译)

【英译】If one can't set up great ambitions and focus on his goals and interests, he won't achieve much even if he studies.

(张夔真 译)

3 【原文】学贵心悟,守旧无功。

《张子全书·经学理窟·义理篇》

【今译】学习贵在用心领悟,因循守旧不会有成就。

(张夔真 译)

【英译】The most valuable thing in learning is to set our hearts on understanding, and it is useless to follow the beaten track.

(肖莉莉 译)

4 【原文】于不疑处有疑,方是进矣。

《张子全书·经学理窟·义理篇》

【今译】在看似没有疑问的地方发现疑问,学问就进步了。

(张夔真 译)

【英译】If we can find doubts where there seems to be no doubt, then our knowledge will be improved.

(张夔真 译)

5 【原文】蒙以养正,使蒙者不失其正,教人者之功也。

《张子全书·正蒙·中正篇》

【今译】对小孩的启蒙教育的目的是培养人的刚直正义之气,让懵懂的孩子不失去刚强的正义之气,这就是教育者的功劳。

(张夔真 译)

【英译】The purpose of children's enlightenment education is to cultivate their integrity and justice. It is the duty of educators to keep innocent children from losing their integrity.

(张夔真 译)

6 【原文】古之小儿,便能敬事长者,与之提携,则两手奉长者之手;问之,掩口而对。盖稍不敬事,便不忠信,故教小儿,且先安详恭敬。

《张子全书·语录钞》

【今译】古时候的小孩子,懂得恭敬地侍奉年长的人,手拉着长者相互搀扶;师长问他事情,就会很礼貌地小声回答。大概因为侍奉师长稍微有不恭敬的话,就是不忠不信,所以教育小孩,首先要教他们举止安详、行事恭敬。

(张夔真 译)

【英译】In ancient times, it was a common sense for children to serve the elderly respectfully. For example, they would support the aged with their hands, and when the teacher asked them something, they would answer politely in a low voice.

Maybe it's because if they show a little disrespect, they will be regarded as disloyal people. Therefore, the first thing we should teach our children is how to behave peacefully and respectfully.

（张媺真 译）

7 【原文】志小则易足,易足则无由进。

《张子全书·经学理窟·学大原下》

【今译】志向短小就容易自满,自满就不会再进取。

（张媺真 译）

【英译】It's easy to be complacent if you are shortsighted, and you won't make progress if you are complacent.

（张媺真 译）

8 【原文】人多是耻于问人。假使今日问于人,明日胜于人,有何不可?

《张子全书·经学理窟·学大原下》

【今译】人们大多会觉得向别人请教是羞耻的。但是,假如今天向他人请教,明天就胜过他人,那么向他人请教有什么不可以的呢?

（张媺真 译）

【英译】Most people feel ashamed to ask others for advice. However, if you ask someone today, you can be better than him tomorrow. Then why not?

（张媺真 译）

9 【原文】教人者必知至学之难易,知人之美恶,当知谁可先传此,谁将后倦此。

《张子全书·正蒙·中正篇》

【今译】教育者一定要知道学业的难易深浅,知道学生的优点和缺点,应当知道可以先传授哪些内容,如果后教哪些内容就会感到厌倦。

（张媺真 译）

【英译】Educators must know the difficulty level of teaching content and the advantages and disadvantages of students. They should know what can be taught first and what will make the students feel bored,if taught later.

（张媺真 译）

10 【原文】为学大益,在自求变化气质。

《张子全书·语录钞》

【今译】学习的最大好处,在于可以潜移默化地改变人的言行风度。

（张媺真 译）

【英译】The biggest advantage of learning is that it can change people's manners of speech and behavior.

（张媺真 译）

11 【原文】教人至难,必尽人之材,乃不误人。

《张子全书·语录钞》

【今译】教育人是最难的事,一定要彻底发挥学生的才能,才不会耽误人才。

（张媺真 译）

【英译】The most difficult thing in the world is to educate people. We must give full play to the students' abilities so as not to hold up their talent.

（张甍真 译）

12 【原文】洪钟未尝有声，由扣乃有声；圣人未尝有知，由问乃有知。

《正蒙·中正篇》

【今译】大钟本身没有声音，因为敲击才会发出声音；圣人也并非生来就是智慧的，因为常向人请教才有了智慧。

（张甍真 译）

【英译】The bell itself has no sound. It makes sound because it is struck. Saints are not intelligent either. They have wisdom because they often ask people for advice.

（张甍真 译）

（十四）程颐 Cheng Yi

1 【原文】共君一夜话，胜读十年书。

《伊川先生语》

【今译】和有智慧的君子一夜谈话，胜过读上十年诗书。

（张甍真 译）

【英译】One evening's conversation with a superior man is worth of study for ten years.

（张甍真 译）

2 【原文】是故觉者约其情，使合于中，正其心，养其性，故曰性其情。愚者则不知制之，纵其情而至于邪僻，梏其性而亡之，故曰情其性。凡学之道，正其心，养其性而已。中正而诚，则圣矣。

《二程文集·颜子所好何学论》

【今译】所以明智的人约束自己的情欲使它合乎正道，同时努力端正思想、修养品性，就叫作"理智战胜自然情感"。愚昧的人却不懂得自我约束，放纵自己的情欲让自己变得乖戾邪恶，以致禁锢了自己的心性，心性就泯灭了，就叫作"情感战胜理性"。学习的方法，就是正心养性。内心中正，真诚信实，就可称为圣人了。

（张甍真 译）

【英译】Therefore, the wise man restrains his desire to make it right, and tries to correct his thought and cultivation, which is called "Reason over Emotion". Ignorant people do not know self-discipline. They indulge their lust, and let themselves become grumpy and evil, resulting in the soul being imprisoned or even dying, which is called "Emotion over Reason". The way to learn is to cultivate the mind. If you are sincere and honest, you can be called a saint.

（张甍真 译）

3 【原文】君子之学，必先明诸心，知所养，然后力行以求至，所谓"自明而诚"也。

《二程文集·颜子所好何学论》

【今译】君子对学习,必须首先使内心明确学习目标,知道修养道德情操,然后身体力行以求到达目的,这就是所说的"明确了方向自然就会努力实行"。

(张夔真 译)

【英译】For learning, the first thing a gentleman must do is to make his heart clear about his learning goal, and to know how to cultivate his moral sentiment. Then he should practice to achieve his goal. This is the saying that "When your goals are set, your steps will be light".

(张夔真 译)

4 【原文】后人不达,以谓"圣本生知,非学可至",而为学之道遂失。不求诸己而求诸外,以博闻强记、巧文丽辞为工,荣华其言,鲜有至于道者。

《二程文集·颜子所好何学论》

【今译】后人不明白,以为圣人本是生而知之,不是学习可以达到的,因此治学的念头就丧失了。不去要求自己内在的修为,而只想求得外物的实现;认为见闻广博,强于记忆,构思精巧,语言华丽就是学问之工,把自己讲话时的言辞修饰得繁复华丽,这种人少有能学得圣人之道的。

(张夔真 译)

【英译】The later generations don't understand that sages know everything through learning rather than being born like this, so they lose the motivation to study hard. They do not seek inner self-cultivation, but only want to achieve external utility. They think that broad knowledge, good memory, ingenious conception and gorgeous language are the best knowledge, so they made their speech rich and ornate. Few such people can learn the way of saints.

(张夔真 译)

5 【原文】习,重习也。时复思绎,浃洽于中,则说(通假字,通"悦")也。以善及人而信从者众,故可乐也。虽乐于及人,不见是而无闷,乃所谓君子。

——《程氏经说·论语解》

【今译】学习,就应该反复学习。时刻反复思考、演绎,学习的东西在心中融会贯通,则是很愉快的事情。把自己的善行推及他人而使信服的追随者众多,所以值得高兴。乐于把善行推及他人,即使当他人不能接受时,也并不烦忧和愤懑,这便是所谓的君子。

(张夔真 译)

【英译】Study means to learn again and again. It's a pleasure to keep thinking and deducing all the time and learn things in your heart. It is gratifying to spread the good deeds to others and have more followers. You will not worry or resent, even if others can not accept what you are willing to pass on to them. This is so called a Junzi(a man of virtue).

(张夔真 译)

（十五）苏轼 Su Shi

1 【原文】故书不厌百回读，熟读深思子自知。

《送安惇秀才失解西归》

【今译】古时的书不厌其烦百遍地诵读，熟读精思自然你就能够懂得古书的精义。

（张囊真 译）

【英译】Ancient books can be read over and over again. If you study earnestly and think carefully, you will be able to understand it.

（张囊真 译）

2 【原文】退笔如山未足珍，读书万卷始通神。

《柳氏二外甥求笔迹》

【今译】磨掉了的笔头堆积起来有如山高，这也不值得称道；只有读了万卷诗书，才能悟得个中的门道。

（张囊真 译）

【英译】It's not praiseworthy that the broken pens are piled up as high as mountains. Only after reading thousands of books can one understand the truth.

（张囊真 译）

3 【原文】生、死、穷、达，不易其操。

《醉白堂记》

【今译】不论面对的是生存或者死亡，得志或者失意，都不改变自己的操守。

（张囊真 译）

【英译】Whether we are facing survival or death, success or failure, we should not change our integrity.

（张囊真 译）

4 【原文】夫为国不可以生事，亦不可以畏事。畏事之弊与生事均。

《因擒鬼章论西羌夏人事宜札子》

【今译】为了国家不能故意制造事端，也不要畏缩怕事，怕事的恶果与生事均等。

（张囊真 译）

【英译】For the sake of our country, we should not deliberately make troubles, nor be afraid of getting into trouble. Being afraid of things is as bad as causing troubles.

（张囊真 译）

5 【原文】我昔家居断还往，著书不复（一作"暇"）窥园葵。

《送安惇秀才失解西归》

【今译】我曾经在家里闭门谢客，拒绝与外人往来，专心致志地著书甚至没有时间去看院子里的植物。

（张囊真 译）

【英译】I used to shut my door and decline visitors. I was so absorbed in writing that I didn't even have time to look at the plants in the yard.

（张奠真 译）

6 【原文】别来十年学不厌，读破万卷诗愈美。

《送任仅通判黄州兼寄其兄孜》

【今译】分别这十年来，你努力学习不倦怠，读书破万卷，诗歌作得更好了。

（张奠真 译）

【英译】For the past ten years, you have an insatiable desire to learn and make great efforts to study. You have read so many volumes of books that you're better at poetry.

（张奠真 译）

7 【原文】成事在理不在势，服人以诚不以言。

《拟进士对御试策》

【今译】事情办成与否不在于是否有强大的权势，而是要符合公理；要使人信服不是依靠空话，而是应该以诚心诚意令人信服。

（张奠真 译）

【英译】Whether things can be accomplished or not doesn't lie in great power and influence, but in conformity with justice; to make people believe is not to rely on empty talk but to make them believe sincerely.

（张奠真 译）

（十六）欧阳修 Ouyang Xiu

1 【原文】玉不琢，不成器；人不学，不知道。

《欧阳永叔集·诲学说》

【今译】玉料不经过琢磨，就不能制成器物；人如果不学习，也就不会懂得道理。

（张奠真 译）

【英译】An uncut gem does not sparkle. A man who does not learn, cannot understand the truth.

（张奠真 译）

2 【原文】有志诚可乐，及时宜自强。

《送惠勤归余杭》

【今译】胸有宏志着实是一件令人高兴的事情，但是还应该要抓紧时间发奋图强。

（张奠真 译）

【英译】It's great indeed to have a great ambition, but we should also seize the time to work hard.

（张奠真 译）

3 【原文】至哉天下乐，终日在几案。

《读书》

【今译】天底下最快乐的事情,莫过于终日伏案读书。

(张龑真 译)

【英译】There's no greater happiness than studying at desk all day long.

(张龑真 译)

4 【原文】乃知读书勤,其乐固无限。

《读书》

【今译】才明白勤奋读书,原来其中的快乐是无限的。

(张龑真 译)

【英译】Till this day do I get to know that the happiness of studying hard is infinite.

(张龑真 译)

5 【原文】忧劳可以兴国,逸豫可以亡身。

《新五代史·伶官传序》

【今译】忧劳国事可以使国家兴盛强大,贪图安逸享乐则会国破身亡。

(张龑真 译)

【英译】Thinking of potential crisis in state affairs can make the country prosperous and strong, while seeking for comfort and pleasure will lead to the destruction of the country.

(张龑真 译)

6 【原文】夫祸患常积于忽微,而智勇多困于所溺。

《新五代史·伶官传序》

【今译】祸患常常是由点点滴滴极小的错误积累而酿成;即使是聪明英勇的人,也多半会因沉溺于某种嗜好,受其迷惑而陷于困穷。

(张龑真 译)

【英译】Misfortune is often caused by the accumulation of small mistakes. Even brave and intelligent people often fall into poverty because of addiction.

(张龑真 译)

7 【原文】夫一,万事之本也,能守一者可以治天下。

《新五代史·一行传》

【今译】专一,是天下万事的根本所在,如果可以保持专一,那么就能够治理天下。

(张龑真 译)

【英译】Concentration is the essence of everything in the world. If you can keep your concentration, you can conquer the world.

(张龑真 译)

8 【原文】酒美春浓花世界,得意人人千万态。
　　　　莫教辜负艳阳天,过了堆金何处买。
　　　　已去少年无计奈,且愿芳心长恁在。
　　　　闲愁一点上心来,算得东风吹不解。

《玉楼春》

【今译】春天处处美酒飘香,春意正浓是花的海洋。人们得意欢欣的样子千姿百态。

不要辜负了如此艳阳天,这样的好时光一旦过去,就是成堆的金子也买不回来。已经逝去的青春年少时光无论如何都回不来了,虽然韶华易逝,但希望年轻的心永不老去。因时光流逝而引发的愁绪在心头,纵使是这春风吹拂也难以消除。

(张冀真 译)

【英译】Spring is full of flowers and wine,
People have different expressions with so much joy.
Don't waste such a sunny day.
Once you let go this beautiful time,
Even piles of gold can't buy it back.
The lost youth has passed away,
And it will not come back as it may.
Though time easily goes by,
I hope my heart will never die.
The sorrow caused by the loss of time is within my mind,
It can not be blowed away by the spring breeze.

(张冀真 译)

9 【原文】春深夜苦短,灯冷焰不长。
尘蠹文字细,病眸涩无光。
坐久百骸倦,中遭群虑戕。
寻前顾后失,得一念十忘。
乃知学在少,老大不可强。

《镇阳读书》节选

【今译】暮春时黑夜短,灯火也不长了。破旧的书被尘土污染、蠹虫蛀坏,上面的字又小,眼睛已经病涩。坐得时间久了,身体也非常困倦。由于年纪大了,前面看过的后面又忘了,记住一句,却忘了十句。于是知道学习最好是在少年时期,年龄大了以后就勉强不得了。

(张冀真 译)

【英译】Time becomes short in late spring night,
Candles glow and give off weak light.
The old books damaged by worms are covered with dust,
words are too small for my sick and sore eyes.
The body feels uncomfortable as I've been sitting for a long time.
Having a mind like a sieve,
I read the front and forgot the back.
So I know that the best time for learning is in the early youth,
It would be too late for the aged to regret.

(张冀真 译)

10 【原文】学校,王政之本也。

《吉州学记》

【今译】学校,是实施仁政的根本。

(肖莉莉 译)

【英译】Schools are the roots of ideal government.

(肖莉莉 译)

(十七) 黄庭坚 *Huang Tingjian*

1 【原文】古之能为文章者,真能陶冶万物,虽取古人之陈言入于翰墨,如灵丹一粒,点铁成金也。

《答洪驹父书》

【今译】古代能写文章的人,能够真正地将万物融于一体,即使引用古人陈旧的话语用在自己的文章中,也能像一粒灵丹妙药,能点铁成金、化腐朽为神奇。

(张冀真 译)

【英译】Great writers in ancient times could truly integrate all things. Even the old words of the ancients are used in their articles, could be like a panacea, turning iron into gold.

(张冀真 译)

2 【原文】三日不读书,便觉语言无味,面目可憎。

《与子飞子均子予书》

【今译】如果三天不读书,就会觉得说出的话没底蕴,连容貌神情都会使人看了厌恶。

(张冀真 译)

【英译】A scholar who hasn't studied for three days would feel that what he said is plain and groundless, and even the appearance can be disgusting.

(张冀真 译)

3 【原文】藏书万卷可教子,遗金满籯常作灾。

《题胡逸老致虚庵》

【今译】藏书万卷可以用来教子,留金满箱往往成为祸灾。

(张冀真 译)

【英译】Ten thousand volumes of books can be collected to teach children, while gold is often left behind to cause disaster.

(张冀真 译)

(十八) 晁说之 *Chao Yuezhi*

1 【原文】为学之道,必本于思。思则得知,不思则不得也。

《晁氏客语》

【今译】治学的方法，必须以思考为本。勤于思考就能获取知识，不思考就得不到知识。

（张奠真 译）

【英译】The method of learning must be based on thinking. Those who are diligent in thinking can gain knowledge; those who do not think can not gain knowledge.

（张奠真 译）

2 【原文】学者有益，须是日新。

《晁氏客语》

【今译】做学问的人要有所进步，必须每天都能学到新知识。

（张奠真 译）

【英译】To make progress, scholars must learn new knowledge every day.

（张奠真 译）

3 【原文】君子莫大于学，莫害于昼，莫病于自足，莫罪于自弃。

《晁氏客语》

【今译】对于君子来说，没有比学习更重要的事情了，最大的危害是停步不前，最大的疾病是骄傲自满，最大的罪过是自暴自弃。

（张奠真 译）

【英译】There is nothing more important than learning for a gentleman. There is nothing more harmful than ceasing to advance. The biggest disease is complacency, while the biggest sin is to abandon oneself.

（张奠真 译）

4 【原文】不思，故有惑；不求，故无得；不问，故不知。

《晁氏客语》

【今译】不思索，所以会有困惑；不追求探索，所以会没有收获；不虚心求问，所以会变得无知。

（张奠真 译）

【英译】Without thinking, there will be confusion; without pursuing, there will be no gains; without asking, there will be ignorance.

（张奠真 译）

（十九）朱熹 Zhu Xi

1 【原文】无一事而不学，无一时而不学，无一处而不学，成功之路也。

《朱子语类》

【今译】没有哪件事情是不需要学习的，没有哪个时间是不能学习的，没有哪处地方是不适合学习的，这就是成功之道。

（张奠真 译）

【英译】Learn whatever it may be; learn whenever you can; and learn wherever you will be. That is the way of success.

（张龑真 译）

2 【原文】读书无疑者，须教有疑；有疑者，却要无疑，到这里方是长进。

《朱子语类》

【今译】读书而没有疑问的人，应该有点怀疑的精神提出疑问；而有疑问的人，却要努力达到最后解决问题，没有疑问，这才是真正长进了。

（张龑真 译）

【英译】If one cannot raise any questions in his reading, he must teach himself to raise questions. If one raises many questions, however, he should learn to solve them. Progress is made through such shifts.

（张龑真 译）

3 【原文】夫童蒙之学，始于衣服冠履，次及言语步趋，次及洒扫涓洁，次及读书写文字，及有杂细事宜，皆所当知。

《童蒙须知》

【今译】儿童启蒙之学，从穿衣戴帽开始，然后是言行举止，再到扫洒清洁，读书写字，以及各种杂事，都是应当懂得的。

（张龑真 译）

【英译】Children's enlightenment education begins with wearing clothes and hats, followed by words and deeds, sweeping and cleaning, reading and handwriting, as well as all kinds of chores.

（张龑真 译）

4 【原文】古之学者为己，欲得之于己也；今之学者为人，欲见知于人也。

《论语精义·卷七下》

【今译】古代的学者学习是为了自身修养，想要自己有所收获；今天的学者学习是为了给别人看，想要别人了解自己。

（张龑真 译）

【英译】Ancient scholars study for their own self-cultivation and want to gain something for themselves; nowadays scholars study for others and want others to understand themselves.

（张龑真 译）

5 【原文】人未安之，又进之，未喻之，又告之，徒使人生此节目。不尽材，不顾安，不由诚，皆是施之妄也。教人至难，必尽人之材，乃不误人。

《近思录·教学》

【今译】学生尚未领会，老师又推进新的教学内容，学生还没弄明白，老师又告诉新的道理，这样就白白地让学生头脑中产生这众多繁琐的项目。不能充分发挥学生的才能，不顾及学生的学习程度，没有激发学生由衷的诚服，这都是盲目实施的教育方法。教育人是非常困难的，必须尽量发挥学生的潜能，才可以不误人子弟。

（张龑真 译）

【英译】Before the students can understand, the teacher has taught the new teaching content and the new truth, which will confuse the students in their minds. If we can't give full play to the students' ability, and inspire their sincere obedience, but ignore their learning level, then it is a blind education method. It's very difficult to educate people. We must give full play to the potential of students so as not to mislead them.

(张奠真 译)

6 【原文】余尝谓:读书有三到,谓心到,眼到,口到。心不在此,则眼不看仔细,心眼既不专一,却只漫浪诵读,决不能记,记亦不能久也。

《训学斋规》

【今译】我曾说过:读书要有"三到",叫做"心到"、"眼到"、"口到"。心思不在读书上,那么眼睛就不会看得仔细,心思和眼睛既然都不专心一意,却只是随随便便地诵读,那一定记不住,即使记住了也不会长久。

(张奠真 译)

【英译】I once said that there should be three things to use in reading a book— the eyes, the mouth, and the mind. If the mind is not focused, then the eyes will not look carefully. If you are not single-minded and just read it casually, you will not remember it. Even if you do, it will not last long.

(张奠真 译)

7 【原文】为学之道,莫先于穷理;穷理之要,必在于读书;读书之法,莫贵于循序而致精;而致精之本,则又在于居敬而持志,此不易之理也。

《朱子全书·甲寅行宫便殿奏札》

【今译】论及做学问的途径,没有什么是比穷究事理更首要的了。穷究事理的要领,必定在于读书;读书的方法,没有比循序渐进而达到精深更可贵的了。而读书要达到精深的根本,则又在于态度严肃认真和保持志向,这是亘古不变的真理。

(张奠真 译)

【英译】Nothing is more important than a thorough inquiry in learning. The key to a thorough inquiry lies in reading books; there is no more valuable ways to read than to proceed in an orderly way. The essence of deep reading lies in serious attitude and keeping ambition, which is the eternal truth.

(张奠真 译)

8 【原文】勿谓今日不学而有来日,勿谓今年不学而有来年。日月逝矣,岁不我延。呜呼老矣,是谁之愆?

《劝学文》

【今译】不要说今天不学习还有明天可以努力学习,不要说今年不学习还有明年可以努力学习。时光流逝啊,岁月不会等我。哀叹自己已经老了,这是谁的错啊?

(张奠真 译)

【英译】Don't say there is another day without learning today. Don't say there is another year without learning this year. Time goes by, and I can not prolong my life. Alas, I get old before I know it, whose fault is this?

(张奠真 译)

（二十）张孝祥 Zhang Xiaoxiang

1 【原文】夫学如积水，其积愈深，则其流愈远。

《于湖居士文集·与冀伯英》

【今译】学习就像积水，积存越深，那么它流得就会越远。

（肖莉莉 译）

【英译】Learning is like accumulated water: the deeper it accumulates, the farther it flows.

（肖莉莉 译）

2 【原文】立志欲坚不欲锐，成功在久不在速。

《论治体札子·甲申二月九日》

【今译】树立志向需要坚定不要急切，成功在于持之以恒而不要急功近利。

（张巘真 译）

【英译】Your goal should be firm, not urgent. Success lies in perseverance, not speed.

（张巘真 译）

3 【原文】学无早晚，但恐始勤终随。

《于湖居士文集·勉过子读书》

【今译】学习不在于起步早晚，只怕开始的时候勤勉而终了的时候随便。

（张巘真 译）

【英译】It doesn't matter whether one starts learning at an early age or an old age.

（张巘真 译）

4 【原文】谁知对床语，胜读十年书。

（《钦夫、子明、定叟夜话舟中，钦夫说〈论语〉数解，天地之心、圣人之心尽在是矣，明日赋诗以别》）

【今译】谁能想到，与友人倾心交谈，收获简直胜过读十年诗书。

（张巘真 译）

【英译】Who would have thought that a few hours of devoted conversation with a friend would be better than ten years of reading and studying.

（张巘真 译）

（二十一）杨时 Yang Shi

1 【原文】今之学者有三弊：溺于文章，牵于训诂，惑于异端。

《二程粹言·论学篇》

【今译】当今做学问的人有三种弊病：沉溺于文章，被训诂所牵制，被旁门左道所迷惑。

（张冀真 译）

【英译】Today's scholars have three disadvantages: being drowned by articles, being bound by exegeses, being confused by heresies.

（张冀真 译）

2 【原文】知过而能改，闻善而能用。

《二程粹言·论学篇》

【今译】发现有过错，就要能改正；听到好建议，就要能采纳。

（张冀真 译）

【英译】If there is a fault, it must be corrected; if there is a good suggestion, it must be adopted.

（张冀真 译）

3 【原文】立志。志立则有本。譬之艺木，由毫末拱把，至于合抱而干云者，有本故也。

《二程粹言·论学篇》

【今译】树立志向。志向确立之后就有了根本。这就好比种树，从小苗长到拱把那样粗，最后变成直上云霄的合抱大树，是因为有根本的缘故。

（张冀真 译）

【英译】Build up your aspiration. Once you have set your aspirations, you have a foundation. It's like planting trees. Growing up from a small sapling, it will eventually become a towering tree, because it has roots.

（张冀真 译）

4 【原文】学者有所闻，而不著乎心，不见乎行，则其所闻固自他人之言耳，于己何与焉？

《二程粹言·论学篇》

【今译】求学的人虽然听闻了老师的教诲，但却不存放在心上，也不见之于行动，他所了解的还是别人的主张，那么对自己又有什么帮助呢？

（张冀真 译）

【英译】Although the students hear the teacher's instructions, they do not pay attention to it or practice it. All they know is what others say. How can it be of any help?

（张冀真 译）

5 【原文】读书将以穷理，将以致用也。今或滞心于章句之末，则无所用也。此学者之大患。

《二程粹言·论学篇》

【今译】读书应该寻根究源，应当学以致用。现在有些人把心力停留在章节句读这些次要问题上，实在没什么用处。这是学者的致命毛病。

（张冀真 译）

【英译】We should study thoroughly and apply what we have learned. Nowadays, some people focus on those irrelevant problems such as sentences and phrases, which is really useless. This is the fatal fault of scholars.

（张奠真 译）

6 【原文】百工治器，必贵于有用。器而不可用，工不为也。学而无所用，学将何为也？

《二程粹言·论学篇》

【今译】各种工匠制作器具，一定注重要有实际用途。器物没有实用价值，工匠是不会制作的。学习而不能加以运用，那么学了还能干什么呢？

（张奠真 译）

【英译】Craftsmen in various industries would pay attention to practicality when making tools. Craftsmen don't make tools that have no practical value. If what you learn cannot be put into practice, what's the use of it?

（张奠真 译）

7 【原文】力学而得之，必充广而行之。不然者，局局其守耳。

《二程粹言·论学篇》

【今译】努力学习而获得知识，一定要在广阔的领域里去运用它。不这样的话，就只是狭隘地局守知识。

（张奠真 译）

【英译】We must make use of the knowledge gained through hard study in a wide range of fields. If not, it's just knowledge.

（张奠真 译）

8 【原文】人之于学，避其所难而姑为其易者，斯自弃也已。夫学者必志于大道，以圣人自期，而犹有不至者焉？

《二程粹言·论学篇》

【今译】有的人对于学习，逃避困难的而暂且只去学容易的，这是自我放弃不求上进而已。学者一定要把志向放在大道上，以圣贤所具有的品质来要求自己，如此还有不能够达到的吗？

（张奠真 译）

【英译】Some people only learn simple things and avoid difficulties in learning. They make no effort to seek progress and give up on themselves. Scholars must have great ambitions and high standards for themselves. If so, there is nothing that can't be achieved.

（张奠真 译）

9 【原文】学者所见所期，不可不远且大也。及夫施于用，则必有其渐。

《二程粹言·论学篇》

【今译】学者所见识到的和所希望的，不能不高远、宏大。等到推行运用时，则必须要循序渐进。

（张奠真 译）

【英译】What scholars have seen should be broad, and what they hope for must be ambitious. When it comes to application, it must proceed step by step in the proper order.

（张奠真 译）

10 【原文】教不立,学不传,人材不期坏而自坏。

《二程粹言·论学篇》

【今译】如果不兴办教育,不传播学问,那么即使不希望人才变坏他自己也要变坏。

(张燕真 译)

【英译】If the government doesn't set up education and spread knowledge, talents will go astray to the contrary of people's expectation.

(张燕真 译)

11 【原文】善学者,当求其所以然之故,不当诵其文,过目而已也。

《二程粹言·论学篇》

【今译】善于学习的人,读书求学时,应当刨根问底、知其所以然,而不应该只是诵读文章,看几眼而已。

(张燕真 译)

【英译】Those who are good at learning should have a thorough understanding of the reasons, rather than only turning over pages and reading articles.

(张燕真 译)

12 【原文】君子之学贵一,一则明,明则有功。

《二程粹言·论学篇》

【今译】君子做学问贵在专一,心志专一才会明晓事理,明晓事理才能有所成就。

(张燕真 译)

【英译】It is important for a gentleman to be single-minded in learning. Only when he is single-minded can he know the reason clearly, and only when he knows the reason clearly can he achieve something.

(张燕真 译)

13 【原文】进学不诚则学杂,处事不诚则事败,自谋不诚则欺心而弃己,与人不诚则丧德而增怨。

《二程粹言·论学篇》

【今译】求学问如果没有诚心,学到的东西势必杂乱无章;做事情如果没有诚心,那么做任何事情都会失败;为自己做打算时没有诚心,那么既欺骗了内心又坑害了自己;和人打交道时如果没有诚心,就会丧失道德,并且增加别人的怨恨。

(张燕真 译)

【英译】Without sincerity, learning is bound to be disorderly; without sincerity, everything will fail; without sincerity, you will deceive and harm yourself; without sincerity, you will lose morality and increase resentment.

(张燕真 译)

14 【原文】耻不知而不问,终于不知而已。以为不知而必求之,终能知之矣。

《二程粹言·论学篇》

【今译】耻于不知道又不虚心请教别人,最终到底还是不知道。认为不懂不明白的就去求教于人,终究能够搞清楚。

(张燕真 译)

【英译】He who will not ask others even if he is ashamed of not knowing, would not know eventually. If one doesn't know something, just ask others, and he will finally find out.

（张奠真 译）

15 【原文】作成人材难,变化人材易。

《二程粹言·论政篇》

【今译】培养一个人才很困难,但是要想毁掉人才却很容易。

（张奠真 译）

【英译】It's difficult to cultivate a talent, but it's easy to destroy one.

（张奠真 译）

（二十二）陆九渊 Lu Jiuyuan

【原文】人之不可以不学,犹鱼之不可以无水！而世至视若赘疣,岂不甚可叹哉？

《陆九渊集·与黄循中》

【今译】人不可以不学习,就像鱼儿不可以没有水！然而世人把求学看成是多余的事情,岂不令人悲叹？

（肖莉莉 译）

【英译】Learning is indispensable to man, just like fish cannot live without water. How lamentable it is that learning is regarded by many as something superfluous!

（肖莉莉 译）

（二十三）罗大经 Luo Dajing

【原文】学不必博,要之有用；仕不必达,要之无愧。

《鹤林玉露》

【今译】不必博学,但要学之有用；当官不必显赫,但要问心无愧。

（肖莉莉 译）

【英译】Learning does not target at erudition but rather usefulness. Being an official does not target at promotion but rather clear conscience.

（肖莉莉 译）

五　元明清时期
Period of the Yuan, Ming and Qing Dynasties

（一）关汉卿 Guan Hanqing

【原文】一日为师,终身为父。

《玉镜台》

【今译】一日是我的老师,终身就是我的父亲。

（肖莉莉 译）

【英译】He who teaches me only one day can be my father for lifelong time.

（肖莉莉 译）

（二）宋濂 Song Lian

【原文】余幼时即嗜学。

《送东阳马生序》

【今译】我年幼时就嗜好读书。

（肖莉莉 译）

【英译】I took delight in reading when I was a little child.

（肖莉莉 译）

（三）罗贯中 Luo Guanzhong

【原文】有道伐无道,无德让有德。

《三国演义》

【今译】正义的讨伐不正义的,没有品德的让贤于品德高尚的。

(肖莉莉 译)

【英译】Those who are righteous against those who are unrighteous, and those devoid of virtue give way to those with virtue.

(肖莉莉 译)

(四) 于谦 Yu Qian

【原文】粉身碎骨全不怕,要留清白在人间。

《石灰吟》

【今译】即便粉身碎骨也不惧怕,情愿把一身清白留在人间。

(肖莉莉 译)

【英译】Though smashed into pieces, one will not be frightened and he'll stay clean in the world.

(肖莉莉 译)

(五) 文嘉 Wen Jia

【原文】我生待明日,万事成蹉跎。

《明日歌》

【今译】如果人的一生都在等待明日,那么他将虚度光阴,一事无成。

(肖莉莉 译)

【英译】If all things are put off till tomorrow, one will idle away his time and get nowhere.

(肖莉莉 译)

(六) 王守仁 Wang Shouren

【原文】志不立,天下无可成之事。

《教条示龙场诸生》

【今译】没有志向,天下什么事也做不成。

(肖莉莉 译)

【英译】Nothing under heaven can be achieved without ambition.

(肖莉莉 译)

（七）王延相 Wang Yanxiang

【原文】学者于贫贱富贵不动其心，死生祸福不变其守。

《慎言》

【今译】求学之人对贫贱富贵毫不动心，面临生死祸福也会坚持操守。

（肖莉莉 译）

【英译】A scholar will not be stirred by poverty or wealth, humbleness or nobility. He will adhere to his personal integrity and not be disturbed by death or life, disaster or happiness.

（肖莉莉 译）

（八）洪应明 Hong Yingming

【原文】攻人之过毋太严，要思其堪受；教人之善毋过高，当使其可从。

《菜根谭》

【今译】指责别人的过错不能太严苛，要考虑别人的承受能力；劝人从善也不能要求太高，应当使他尽力而为。

（肖莉莉 译）

【英译】When blaming one for his faults, do not be too harsh, and his bearing capacity should be considered. When instructing one to follow a virtuous path, do not set too demanding goals, and what he is capable of accomplishing should be considered.

（肖莉莉 译）

（九）《增广贤文》 Zengguang Xianwen

1　【原文】集韵增广，多见多闻。

《增广贤文》

【今译】搜集押韵的文字汇编而成"增广"，能使你见多识广。

（肖莉莉 译）

【英译】This expanded poetic collection can broaden your sights and sounds.

（肖莉莉 译）

2　【原文】相识满天下，知心能几人。

《增广贤文》

【今译】和我相识的人到处都是,可知心的人儿却没有几个。

（肖莉莉 译）

【英译】My acquaintances are all over the world, but the real intimates are rare.

（肖莉莉 译）

3 【原文】读书须用意,一字值千金。

《增广贤文》

【今译】读书须用心投入,才能文采出众,一字千金。

（肖莉莉 译）

【英译】Only one learns by heart can his single word be worth a thousand pieces of gold.

（肖莉莉 译）

4 【原文】钱财如粪土,仁义值千金。

《增广贤文》

【今译】钱财就如粪土一般低贱和微不足道,而仁义道德则价值千金。

（肖莉莉 译）

【英译】Money and wealth are as worthless as dirt, while virtue and morality are worth their weight in gold.

（肖莉莉 译）

5 【原文】一年之计在于春,一日之计在于晨。

《增广贤文》

【今译】一年的计划要在春天安排好,一天的计划要在早晨安排好。

（肖莉莉 译）

【英译】A good start in the spring decides a whole year's work, a good start in the morning decides a whole day's work.

（肖莉莉 译）

6 【原文】一寸光阴一寸金。

《增广贤文》

【今译】光阴宝贵,堪比黄金。

（肖莉莉 译）

【英译】An inch of time is worth an inch of gold.

（肖莉莉 译）

7 【原文】万般皆下品,唯有读书高。

《增广贤文》

【今译】世间所有行业都是低下的,只有读书才是高尚的。

（肖莉莉 译）

【英译】Nothing is lofty except reading books.

（肖莉莉 译）

8 【原文】与君一席话,胜读十年书。

《增广贤文》

【今译】与对方的交谈受益很大,胜过读了十年的诗书。

（肖莉莉 译）

【英译】A talk with a learned friend can benefit one more than ten school years.

（肖莉莉 译）

9 【原文】书到用时方恨少,事非经过不知难。

《增广贤文》

【今译】等到真正用到知识的时候才后悔自己读的书太少了;很多事情如果不是亲身经历过,就不知道它有多难。

（肖莉莉 译）

【英译】One will not regret his meager reading until he puts it to use, and one fails to know the hardness of life except through personal experience.

（肖莉莉 译）

(十) 李贽 *Li Zhi*

1 【原文】学问须时时拈掇,乃时时受用,纵无人讲,亦须去寻人讲。

《焚书·答庄纯夫书》

【今译】做学问要时时与人交流、对话,从中受益,才每时每刻都能受用,即便是没有人可以交流,也应当去寻找志趣相投、心灵相通的挚友论谈。

（张冀真 译）

【英译】Learning should be frequently renewed, so that it can be used all the time. You should seek opportunities to share it with other people, even if you seem to have no chance to talk to others about it.

（张冀真 译）

2 【原文】能自立者必有骨也。

《焚书·荀卿李斯误吴公》

【今译】能够自立自强的人必定有骨气。

（张冀真 译）

【英译】Those who are able to stand on their own must have great integrity.

（张冀真 译）

3 【原文】常知足则常足,故富;能脱俗则不俗,故贵。

《焚书·富莫富于常知足》

【今译】经常能知道满足的人,就会长久地满足,因此会富有;能够超脱凡俗的人就不会落入庸俗,所以会尊贵。

（张冀真 译）

【英译】A contented person will always feel satisfied, so he/she will be rich. A detached person will not fall into the vulgarity, so he/she will be respected.

（张冀真 译）

4 【原文】能下人,故其心虚;其心虚,故所取广;所取广,故其人愈高。

《焚书·高洁说》

【今译】一个人能够居人之下,才能虚心;能够虚心了,所获得的才能更多更广;所得的更加广泛,所以才能够成为人上人。

(张冀真 译)

【英译】Those who can humble themselves can be modest; only those who can be modest can gain more; only those who gain more can become the best men among people.

(张冀真 译)

5 【原文】物不经锻炼,终难成器;人不得切琢,终不成人。

《焚书·答耿司寇》

【今译】器物不经过冶炼,终将难以成为名器;人不经过教育(打磨),终将不能成为人才。

(张冀真 译)

【英译】Without smelting, artifacts will not be molded; without education, people will not become talents.

(张冀真 译)

(十一) 王骥德 Wang Jide

1 【原文】天下无难事,只怕有心人。

《题红记》

【今译】天下没有所谓的难事,只要有毅力和决心,就没有什么办不到的事情。

(肖莉莉 译)

【英译】Nothing is impossible for those who have perseverance and determination.

(肖莉莉 译)

(十二) 董其昌 Dong Qichang

【原文】读万卷书,行万里路。

《画禅室随笔·卷二·画诀》

【今译】读书万卷,扩大涉猎范围;行路万里,凡事亲自躬行实践。

(肖莉莉 译)

【英译】Read as thousands of books as one can, and travel as thousands of miles as one can.

(肖莉莉 译)

(十三) 黄宗羲 Huang Zongxi

【原文】学者志不立，一经患难，愈见消沮，所以先要立志。

《宋元学案》

【今译】求学之人不立志，一旦遇到困难祸端，就会愈发消沉沮丧，所以首要之事就是立志。

（肖莉莉 译）

【英译】A scholar who has not set up ambition inclines to be depressed and dispirited when he encounters difficulties and misfortunes. Hence the first and foremost thing is to set up ambition.

（肖莉莉 译）

(十四) 顾炎武 Gu Yanwu

1 【原文】君子之为学也，非利己也。

《亭林余集》

【今译】君子做学问，并非为了一己之私。

（肖莉莉 译）

【英译】When Junzi(a man of virtue) devotes to learning, he does not target at benefiting himself.

（肖莉莉 译）

2 【原文】天下兴亡，匹夫有责。

《日知录》

【今译】国家的兴盛与衰亡，是每一个普通老百姓的责任。

（肖莉莉 译）

【英译】Everyone is responsible for the rise and fall of his country.

（肖莉莉 译）

(十五) 王夫之 Wang Fuzhi

【原文】才以用而日生，思以引而不竭。

《周易外传》

【今译】人的才干在锻炼使用中日渐增长，人的思维因为经常思考才不会枯竭。

（肖莉莉 译）

【英译】One's talent gets refreshed in daily active use, and one's thoughts will not be exhausted by constant thinking.

（肖莉莉 译）

（十六）朱柏庐 Zhu Bailu

1 【原文】一粥一饭，当思来处不易；半丝半缕，恒念物力维艰。

《朱子家训》

【今译】对于一碗粥或一顿饭，我们也要想着它来之不易；对于衣服的半根丝或半缕线，我们心里也要常念着这些物资的生产是很艰难的。

（肖莉莉 译）

【英译】When you eat your food, you ought to bear in mind that it is not easy to grow crops; when you wear clothes, you ought to remember that every material of your clothing is difficult to produce.

（肖莉莉 译）

2 【原文】宜未雨而绸缪，毋临渴而掘井。

《朱子家训》

【今译】凡事要先准备，没下雨的时候就要先把房子修葺完善，不要到口渴的时候才去掘井。

（肖莉莉 译）

【英译】Do not have the cloak to make when it begins to rain. Do not wait to dig a well until you are thirsty.

（肖莉莉 译）

3 【原文】子孙虽愚，经书不可不读。

《朱子家训》

【今译】子孙虽然愚笨，但经书也是不可不读的。

（肖莉莉 译）

【英译】All my offspring should read books even if they are clumsy.

（肖莉莉 译）

（十七）张履祥 Zhang Lüxiang

1 【原文】大凡为学，必须立志。志大而大，志小而小。

《初学备忘》

【今译】凡是致力于做学问的，必须先树立志向。志向大成就也就大，志向小成就也就小。

（肖莉莉 译）

【英译】One who devotes himself to learning must set up ambition first and foremost. A far ambition paves way for great achievements; a slight ambition contributes to small achievement.

（肖莉莉 译）

2 【原文】有有志而不遂者矣，未有无志而成者。

《初学备忘》

【今译】拥有志向而不能成就大业，这是曾经有的；没有志向而能成就大业，这是不曾有的。

（肖莉莉 译）

【英译】There are some who have ambition but still fail to achieve great accomplishments; but there is no one who can achieve great accomplishments without any ambition.

（肖莉莉 译）

（十八）颜元 Yan Yuan

【原文】学而必习，习而必行。

《习斋言行录》

【今译】学习之后必须要复习，复习之后必须要实践。

（肖莉莉 译）

【英译】Reviewing should closely follow leaning, and practice should closely follow reviwing.

（肖莉莉 译）

（十九）李毓秀 Li Yuxiu

1 【原文】读书法，有三到，心眼口，信皆要。

《弟子规》

【今译】读书的方法有三处要领：眼到、口到、心到。三者缺一不可，如此方可事半功倍。

（肖莉莉 译）

【英译】There are three take-away points in ways of reading. You should have a good use of your eyes, mouth and heart. These three jointly contribute to the best effect.

（肖莉莉 译）

2 【原文】心有疑，随札记，就人问，求确义。

《弟子规》

【今译】求学过程中,如果心存疑问,应随时记笔记,一有机会就向别人请教,以求明白确切的含义。

(肖莉莉 译)

【英译】If you have doubts when learning, you should always take notes so that you can consult others to shed light to the exact meaning.

(肖莉莉 译)

(二十) 张潮 Zhang Chao

1 【原文】涉猎虽曰无用,犹胜于不通古今。

《幽梦影》

【今译】博览群书虽不能学有所长,但胜于不通古今。

(肖莉莉 译)

【英译】Desultory and extensive browsing are better than not being acquainted with books at all.

(肖莉莉 译)

2 【原文】有工夫读书,谓之福。

《幽梦影》

【今译】能够有工夫读书,可谓是一种福气。

(肖莉莉 译)

【英译】Having time for reading can be seen as a blessing.

(肖莉莉 译)

3 【原文】发前人未发之论,方是奇书。

《幽梦影》

【今译】能够提出前人不曾提出的论点,才称得上是奇书。

(肖莉莉 译)

【英译】Master pieces are those which make arguments that no one has made before.

(肖莉莉 译)

4 【原文】喜读书者不以忙闲作辍。

《幽梦影》

【今译】喜欢读书的人不以有无空闲作为没时间读书的借口。

(肖莉莉 译)

【英译】A book lover does not cease reading on the excuse of no time to read.

(肖莉莉 译)

5 【原文】凡事不宜刻,若读书则不可不刻。

《张潮·幽梦影》

【今译】凡事都不宜于过于苛刻,但读书不可以不刻苦。

(肖莉莉 译)

【英译】One must not be fastidious about anything except in reading books.

（肖莉莉 译）

6 【原文】天下无书则已，有则必当读。

《幽梦影》

【今译】天下没有书便罢了，有书就一定要读。

（肖莉莉 译）

【英译】If there were no books, we had no other choice but to sigh, but if there are books, we will definitely be thirsty for reading.

（肖莉莉 译）

（二十一）张伯行 Zhang Boxing

1 【原文】学者功夫不勤苦，而欲有所得，犹农夫不耕耘，而望有获也。

《困学录集粹》

【今译】学习的人不勤奋刻苦学习，工夫不到，却想要有所收获，就像是农夫不播种耕作，就希望能够有所收获一样。

（张夔真 译）

【英译】Diligence is indispensable to a scholar, who expects to obtain knowledge, just as cultivating is indispensable to a farmer, who expects to reap harvest.

（张夔真 译）

2 【原文】吾人为学，须是朝乾夕惕，日有孳孳。不肯稍自宽假，真见得一息尚存，此志不容稍懈。

《困学录集粹》

【今译】我们努力修习学问的人，必须要终日勤勉谨慎，努力不懈。不肯稍微有半点儿懈怠，只要还有一口气，这个志向就不容许略微松懈一点儿。

（张夔真 译）

【英译】We who strive to learn must be diligent, and prudent all day long. As long as there is a breath, We dare not slack off a little bit.

（张夔真 译）

3 【原文】圣人之所以为圣也，只是好学下问。

张伯行辑订《朱子语类辑略》

【今译】圣人之所以圣明贤德，只是因为他们勤于学习不耻下问。

（张夔真 译）

【英译】The reason why sages are wise and virtuous is that they are diligent in learning.

（张夔真 译）

4 【原文】教子弟者，自其幼而教之，则甚易；迨其长而始教之，则甚难。幼而教之，使顺其性之本然，故易。长而教之，习染既深，使返其性之本然，故难。

《困学录集粹》

【今译】教育子弟,从他们幼小的时候进行教育,就很容易;等到他们长大才开始教育,就非常困难。幼小时教导他们,使他们顺从本性发展,因此容易;长大以后再教育,因受到外界熏染而养成的习性已经很深了,要使他们恢复到原有的禀性来发展,因此困难。

（张燮真 译）

【英译】It is very easy to teach children when they are young so that they can develop in accordance with their nature; it is very difficult to educate them when they grow up and develop their habits because they are deeply influenced by the outside world.

（张燮真 译）

5 【原文】水之积也厚,则负大舟为有力;德之积也厚,则建大业为有本。

《困学录集粹》

【今译】如果河水积聚深厚,那么负载大船就很有力量;如果道德积聚深厚,那么建立大业就有了基础。

（张燮真 译）

【英译】The river carries great power because of the depth of the water. A great cause can be established because of the accumulation of morality.

（张燮真 译）

6 【原文】天地生人,无不与之以善;圣贤教人,只是与人为善。

《困学录集粹》

【今译】大自然让人们生活在这天地之中,无不赋予人以善良之心;圣贤之师教导人们,只是要让人们行善良之事。

（张燮真 译）

【英译】Nature has given people a kind heart and let people live in this world; the sage enlightens people and let people do good deeds.

（张燮真 译）

7 【原文】书不记,熟读可记;义不精,细思可精。

《学规类编》

【今译】读书记不住,反复熟读就可以记住;意义搞不清楚,仔细思考就可以弄明白。

（张燮真 译）

【英译】If you can't memorize it, you can remember it by reading it over and over again. If you can't figure out the meaning, you can figure it out by thinking it over and over again.

（张燮真 译）

7 【原文】一丝一粒,我之名节;一厘一毫,民之脂膏。宽一分,民受赐不止一分;取一文,我为人不值一文。谁云交际之常,廉耻实伤;倘非不义之财,此物何来?

《禁止馈送檄》

【今译】一丝一粒,都关系到我的名声和操守;一厘一毫,都来自百姓的民脂民膏。对百姓宽松一分,老百姓得到的好处就不止一分;多拿一文,我的为人就一文不值。不要说这只是正常的交际来往,实在是伤廉耻的事;假如这些不是不义之财的话,这些东西又是从何处来的呢?

(张龑真 译)

【英译】Every single thing is related to my reputation and integrity; every little bit comes from the sweat and blood of the people. If we loose our policy towards the people, they will benefit more than a little. If I take more than a penny, then I will be worthless for who I am. Don't ever say that it's just normal social intercourse! It's really a matter of shame. If these are not unjust gains, where do these things come from?

(张龑真 译)

(二十二) 彭端淑 Peng Duanshu

【原文】天下事有难易乎? 为之,则难者亦易矣;不为,则易者亦难矣。人之为学有难易乎? 学之,则难者亦易矣;不学,则易者亦难矣。

《为学一首示子侄》

【今译】天下的事情有困难和容易之分吗? 只要肯做,那么困难的事情也会变得容易;如果不肯做,那么容易的事情也变得困难了。人们做学问有困难和容易之分吗? 只要肯学,那么再难也变得容易了;如果不学,那么再容易也变得困难了。

(肖莉莉 译)

【英译】Is there anything difficult or easy for us to do in the world? If we do it, the difficult thing will become easy; if we don't, the easy thing will appear difficult. Is there anything difficult or easy for learning in the world? If we learn it, the difficult thing will become easy; if we don't, the easy thing will appear difficult.

(肖莉莉 译)

(二十三) 刘岩 Liu Yan

【原文】有书堆数仞,不如读盈寸。

《杂诗》

【今译】藏书众多,但却束之高阁,还不如涉猎虽少却能研读。

(肖莉莉 译)

【英译】To own piles of books of feet high is no better than just read thoroughly one of them.

(肖莉莉 译)

(二十四)袁枚 Yuan Mei

【原文】万卷山积,一篇吟成。

《续诗品·博习》

【今译】只有读书万卷,积累学问,才能写出一首好诗。

(肖莉莉 译)

【英译】It is only after one has read thousands of volumes that he can write a good poem.

(肖莉莉 译)

(二十五)方东树 Fang Dongshu

【原文】君子取人贵恕,及论学术,则不得不严。

《昭昧詹言》

【今译】君子对人贵在宽恕,但论及做学问,则不得不有一个严格的标准。

(肖莉莉 译)

【英译】Junzi(a man of virtue) ought to be forgiving to others, but when it comes to scholarship, he has to set a strict standard.

(肖莉莉 译)

(二十六)龚自珍 Gong Zizhen

1 【原文】落红不是无情物,化作春泥更护花。

《己亥杂诗》

【今译】落花并非无情之物,落在土里化作春泥,还可以培育花儿成长。

(肖莉莉 译)

【英译】Fallen flowers are not unfeeling. Though turned into spring mud, they still nurture the growth of flowers.

(肖莉莉 译)

2 【原文】我劝天公重抖擞,不拘一格降人才。

《己亥杂诗》

【今译】我奉劝上天要重新振作精神,不要拘泥于一种标准,使更多的人才降生。

(肖莉莉 译)

【英译】I urge the heaven to brace up again, and send us more talents without sticking to any fixed pattern.

(肖莉莉 译)

（二十七）魏源 *Wei Yuan*

1 【原文】学问之道，其得之不难者，失之必易。

《魏源集·默觚》

【今译】倘若论学，不难学到的东西，失去必定也容易。

（肖莉莉 译）

【英译】When it comes to leaning, the most easily acquired can be the easiest to forget.

（肖莉莉 译）

2 【原文】不知人之短，不知人之长，不知人长中之短，不知人短中之长，则不可以用人，不可以教人。

《魏源集·默觚》

【今译】不知道别人的短处，也不知道别人的长处，不知道别人的长处之中亦隐藏有短处，也不知道别人的短处之中亦隐藏有长处，这样的话不谙用人之道，也不可以教导他人。

（肖莉莉 译）

【英译】If one is unaware of other people's weak points and strong points, their weak points hidden behind the strong points, and their strong points covered by the weak points, he will fail to manage the personnel or instruct others.

（肖莉莉 译）

（二十八）曾国藩 *Zeng Guofan*

1 【原文】百尺之楼，基于平地；千丈之帛，一尺一寸之所积也。

《曾文正公全集·杂著》

【今译】百尺高的大楼也是从平地而起的，千丈长的锦帛也是一尺一寸积累而来的。

（肖莉莉 译）

【英译】A mansion starts with its foundation, and silk of a thousand meters long accumulates the weaving of every thread.

（肖莉莉 译）

2 【原文】古之成大业者，多自克勤小物而来。

《曾文正公全集·杂著》

【今译】自古以来成就大业的人，大多是勤勉踏实做好每一件小事，严以自律把控每一个小节。

（肖莉莉 译）

【英译】Since ancient times, those who made great achievements always deal with trifles with diligence and self-discipline.

（肖莉莉 译）

3 【原文】天下事当于大处著眼,小处下手。

《曾文正公全集·杂著》

【今译】天下之事应将大事了然于胸,从大事上着眼,但从小事上着手办理。

（肖莉莉 译）

【英译】One ought to have a comprehensive picture of the whole but begin with the trivial parts.

（肖莉莉 译）

（二十九）刘蓉 Liu Rong

1 【原文】一室之不治,何以天下家国为?

《习惯说》

【今译】连一间自己的屋子都不能整理好,凭什么能治理好国家呢?

（肖莉莉 译）

【英译】How can one govern the state well when he cannot keep his own little room tidy?

（肖莉莉 译）

2 【原文】故君子之学贵乎慎始。

《习惯说》

【今译】所以说君子做学问,最可贵的就是开始时谨慎。

（肖莉莉 译）

【英译】Hence the most valuable thing in learning for Junzi(a man of virtue) is to be cautious in the very beginning.

（肖莉莉 译）

参考文献 Works Cited

[1] 蔡希勤. 老人家说系列丛书:管子说[M]. 北京:华语教学出版社,2012.
[2] 刘勰. 文心雕龙[M] 杨国斌,英译;周振甫,今译. 北京:外语教学与研究出版社, 2003.12.
[3] 刘士聪,谷启楠. 中国古代经典名句英译[M]. 北京:商务印书馆,2012.
[4] 颜之推. 颜氏家训(汉英对照)[M]. 宗福常,英译. 北京:外文出版社,2004.01.
[5] 尹邦彦,尹海波. 中国历代名人名言双语对照[M]. 南京:译林出版社,2009.06.
[6] 周秉钧,大中华文库汉英对照:尚书[M]理雅各,英译. 长沙:湖南人民出版社,2013.